Resurrecting Your Life

Dr. Jerry Weber

authorHOUSE

AuthorHouse™
1663 Liberty Drive
Bloomington, IN 47403
www.authorhouse.com
Phone: 1 (800) 839-8640

© 2018 Dr. Jerry Weber. All rights reserved.

No part of this book may be reproduced, stored in a retrieval system, or transmitted by any means without the written permission of the author.

Published by AuthorHouse 10/05/2018

ISBN: 978-1-5462-6220-6 (sc)
ISBN: 978-1-5462-6219-0 (e)

Print information available on the last page.

Any people depicted in stock imagery provided by Getty Images are models, and such images are being used for illustrative purposes only. Certain stock imagery © Getty Images.

This book is printed on acid-free paper.

Because of the dynamic nature of the Internet, any web addresses or links contained in this book may have changed since publication and may no longer be valid. The views expressed in this work are solely those of the author and do not necessarily reflect the views of the publisher, and the publisher hereby disclaims any responsibility for them.

Scripture taken from The Holy Bible, King James Version. Public Domain

Dedicated to my best friend, wife and partner for life – Ann. She has stood next to me for the last 43 years through the good times and the bad as we travel this journey together helping each other grow. She has allowed me the freedom to live my God-given dreams. She gives me the encouragement, love and the most important thing in life every person needs – she believes in me.

"If you **bring forth what is within you**, what you bring forth will save you. If you do *not* bring forth what is within you, what you do not bring forth will destroy you.

Attributed to Jesus from The Gospel of Matthew

Thank you for selecting <u>Resurrecting Your Life</u>. This book can be just another book on your list of books that you have read or you can **use it to help you find what you are looking for** – what everybody is searching for – some truth that your soul connects to. Although we might be on different paths, all of us are heading toward the same destination – God. The difference is how long it takes for us to **discover the secret to happiness and true success**.

<u>Resurrecting Your Life</u> was written to help you **be the best that you can be**. Whether you want to **skim the book, read it** or **take it to a personal level** for the most impact, it is your choice. The following are suggestions of different approaches to reading <u>Resurrecting Your Life</u>.

1) **Allow the Holy Spirit to direct your reading. Hold the book, close your eyes, meditate in silence for a moment, thank God and then just open the book wherever you feel like opening it. Focus on the first paragraph or page and read it for the day. It's a great way to stay inspired.**
2) **Fast Read – If you don't have the time to read the entire book read the words or phrases in bold. They have been specially designed so the reader**

quickly understands the important thought on that page without reading the entire page. This technique, called *'imperative imprinting',* **also works when you are reading the entire book by impressing onto the subconscious mind these powerful positive messages.**

3) After you have read the entire book as it is written, return to The Beginning (the first chapter) This time change all the pronouns such as 'you' to 'I'. This change to a more personal perception is powerful.

However, you choose to **read <u>Resurrecting Your Life</u>** makes no difference. The message is the same. I remember when I showed our son, Michael, the first copy of the book. After looking through the book from front to back cover he asked, "what if I read it starting in the back to the front?"

I stood there, silent, pleasantly surprised by our son asking such "an old soul question." I just answered by repeating what my inner voice clearly whispered to me, "the truth is truth – no matter how you look at it."

Enjoy <u>Resurrecting Your Life</u> however you want to "look at it."

Contents

Introduction xvii

Dr. Weber reflects over the twenty years since he first published this book and how this now proven system has personally helped him live a life he could have only dreamed.

The Gift xxiii

Learn about two incredible spiritual gifts this book received and is sharing with you. Discover the twenty-year old secret about the origin of the front cover. Don't miss the unbelievable image of Jesus that appears on the back cover!

Chapter 1   In The Beginning 1

This chapter challenges you to examine your beliefs about God and Jesus. The chapter's content is based from the Biblical scripture that in the beginning was God and basically God is all. Because this energy of creation is everything and everywhere it is imperative for a person to know the truth because the truth will set them free.

Chapter 2   The Awakening **8**

The concept of resurrection is introduced. The comparison of Jesus's resurrection and the type of resurrection each of us must experience to come back to life and escape the walking dead is discussed. The book outlines a step by step program to find passion and direction again and come back to life.

Chapter 3   Love Is The Answer **20**

Once again, this chapter reminds us that this universal energy is where the secret lies. Love is the answer and all of us know it, but do we live it? Learn how to use the Positive Power of God (love) in everything you do and live with passion.

Chapter 4   The Challenge **31**

Learn why finding your God-given passion is important for you to live your best. You must have a reason to live and love. The challenge is to wake up from sleepwalking through life and take action toward fulfilling your God-given desires.

Chapter 5   I Have A Dream... Do You? 43

This chapter helps you get started on your journey of resurrection. The concept of "re-minding" is discussed which is another important step of bringing back to the mind the dream that you once possessed.

Chapter 6   Vision Quest... 57

Learn how to reconstruct your dreams using The Dream Sheet. Discover how to break through procrastination. Be inspired to take back your dream and never quit until you accomplish it.

Chapter 7   Ask And You Shall Receive...If... 68

Master the art of manifesting your desires by setting goals with God as your co-creator and working those goals. Learn how to use The 5 Steps To Great Goal Setting to help you turn your dreams and desires into reality.

Chapter 8   Seek and Ye Shall Find 74

Discover the power of your subconscious mind and how to use it to build the life that will resurrect you. This invisible "silent partner" will work endlessly to help you achieve your dream if it knows exactly what you desire and it is in the highest divine order.

Chapter 9   It All Comes Down To Attitude............... 83

The concept of attitude is discussed. What is attitude? Why is it so important? Attitude does determine altitude so take a check up from the neck up and stop your stinking thinking and you will be resurrected.. If you need some help eliminating some negative thoughts this chapter can help you.

Chapter 10 You Can Change... 97

What would you do if you knew you couldn't fail? That is the question discussed in this chapter. Many suggestions are given with examples of how to start changing your life to a more empowered, connected person.

Chapter 11 You Must Believe 120

Belief is one of the most important concepts that you must understand and do to resurrect your life. If you don't believe in a higher divine energy called God and the God-given ability you possess it will be impossible to be resurrected. Without belief you will not have the faith to take action. Dr. Weber shares his experience of how to increase your belief.

Chapter 12 Don't Give Up – Get Up!.......................... 133

The reason many people are the "walking dead" is they have lost hope. They have given up. The message in this chapter is don't ever give up on your dreams. By reframing problems to opportunities and challenges the reader will learn empowering techniques to take action and face the obstacles.

Chapter 13 Turning Fear Into Power 149

Fear is what stops most people from living the life they dream. Learn how to turn fear into a friend. By understanding what fear really is you will be able to take the necessary steps to break through the illusion of fear.

Chapter 14 Modeling the Master 167

Jesus said, "Follow me." That is exactly what this chapter teaches. By using the NLP technique of "modeling" the reader learns how to model the best holistic health coach - Jesus

Chapter 15 Thoughts are Things 178

Thoughts control our lives. To resurrect our lives, we must learn how to think differently. The only way to change your life is to change how you think.

Chapter 16 Being Balanced in an Unbalanced World 194

The Wheel of Balance is introduced in this chapter as a perfect tool to help you do a self-evaluation of your life and a step-by-step program to get your life more balanced.

Chapter 17 The Greatest Story Ever Told 211

Be bold and be brave. That is the message in this chapter and the secret of how to be the greatest story ever told. All of us have a God-given gift but the ones who we will remember are the ones who have the courage to live their God-given gifts.

Afterthoughts... 221

A collection of thoughts from Dr. Weber to conclude Resurrecting Your Life.

Introduction

I can't believe it's been twenty years since I wrote this book. It seems as though it has taken me those twenty years to "prove" that the concepts of Resurrecting Your Life truly work.

I have been not only the writer but also a student of this book. After two decades of reading and working with the teachings in this book I have been able to turn my life around for my family. My success has resulted from what I have learned by writing, studying and using these words.

When I was given the idea of writing Resurrection (which was the book title when it was originally published) it was obviously an outlet for me. In 1995 our wonderful life which we had built for over twenty years crashed and we lived on the brink of bankruptcy. As I tell this story in the book, you will see that what we experienced and the things we learned were invaluable. Through these trying times I started writing down my ideas – a pep talk to myself. The manuscript, written out on legal pads, was originally called Don't Give Up, Get Up. I now look back and know that this motivating title was for me.

My original goal in publishing <u>Resurrection</u> was 'to help at least one person.' I felt that if it truly helped at least one person it was a success. Although the book has helped many people, I believe that 'one person' was me. I hope you feel the same personal connection to these words as I have experienced.

In the early years of the book's formation – when the title was still **<u>Don't</u> <u>Give</u> <u>Up</u>, <u>Get</u> <u>Up</u>**, Ann and I had some spiritual experiences that changed our lives forever. After these special soul awakening events, which I discuss in the book (The Gift), I was compelled to change the title and picture on the front cover.

Putting a picture of Jesus on the front cover caused some 'problems' for the book. I was banned from my local public library from speaking about my book because it had a 'religious' figure's picture on the front cover. It was suggested again to change the front cover to 'make it easier.' I absolutely refused to take this beautiful picture of Jesus off the front cover. In my mind that was like rejecting Jesus – not standing up for what I believed.

As my natural health practice exploded I realized that many of my patients needed as much coaching on the emotional, mental and spiritual level as they needed on just a physical level. And because I understood that 'wholistic' health is the entire body and not just physical, I introduced my Holistic Health Coaching program. As I started my coaching sessions I realized that my book - <u>Resurrection</u> was the perfect book for my patients to use as a tool to help them on their path to personal development.

But, there was one problem. The picture of Jesus on the front cover didn't go along with such a thing as Holistic Health Coaching - or did it? After thinking about it I knew that the picture of Jesus was perfect. Who would make a better holistic health coach than Jesus? Once that decision was made then I knew I had to once again change the title to fit its new position. <u>Resurrecting</u> <u>Your</u> <u>Life</u> was decided upon as the new title. That said it all and showed what my life and this book is about.

<u>Resurrecting</u> <u>Your</u> <u>Life</u> has been written to help any human being who is looking for more and who is a truth seeker. These words will ring true to a person who knows they have more to give. These words will make your soul be happy and sing. If you are one of those people and you feel the time is right for you to be all you can be, this book is for you.

The original book - Resurrection has already helped many people who were looking for inspiration and direction to make their lives more complete. I believe that if you live by these words as I have, Resurrecting Your Life can bring more success and happiness into your life then you have ever dreamed possible! Believe!

Using these concepts, I turned my life around. I now work as a successful, board-certified Naturopath doctor and Holistic Health Coach. I love helping people with their health while discovering who they truly are. I assist them in discovering their God-given potential while supporting them as a doctor, coach and friend as they blossom in all areas of their lives. I now understand how powerful these words are and how they can **change someone's life**.

Another reason that I changed the book's title from Resurrection to Resurrecting Your Life is that over these last twenty years, not only the book, but also I have changed. What started out as a motivational, inspirational self-help book has now transformed into our official book used in our Holistic Health Coaching program. How you use it will be your choice. I would like to share one story how one of my friends used the book to better his life.

When the first copy of <u>Resurrection</u> was released I was still working as a hairdresser. Carl was one of my clients whom I saw every month. Carl and I attended high school together but had not seen each other for many years. Talking to him I discovered that he wasn't happy. After high school Carl had moved to Seattle, got married and had a daughter. Things didn't work out between him and his wife so they divorced, and Carl moved back home. I could tell that Carl missed his daughter who was now twenty years old. He wanted to move back and see her but had been stuck for years working in a factory.

As I cut Carl's hair I was excited about releasing my newly self-published book. I suggested that he should buy a copy and read it. After a few months of coaxing, he finally decided to purchase it. At his next appointment I asked Carl if he had read my book and he answered, "no, but it is lying right there on my coffee table. I see it every morning."

I was a little disappointed that I couldn't even get him interested enough to read it. Every time that Carl came in for his monthly haircut I would ask and I would receive the same answer. One day Carl called me, and I could tell something was different just by hearing the excitement in his voice. I asked him if he needed a haircut and I received a wonderful surprise. He said, "That would be a little hard to do. I moved back to Seattle! My daughter is now twenty-one and we have reunited. It is wonderful. Thank you."

Well of course, I had to ask the obvious question hoping that my book helped this abrupt change of thinking. "Sounds like you read my book," I stated proudly to him. He answered, "no, I just looked at the front cover every day and just that kept reminding me what you said."

An update to this story is that Carl and I reconnected on Facebook and he actually sent me a message that read… "<u>Resurrection</u> changed my life."

Writing and reading this book changed my life. I know that it can **change your life** and give you the tools to **make your dreams come true**.

Health is wealth. May you **prosper**.
Dr. Jerry Weber, N.D.
May 19, 2018

The Gift

I still remember the day that this book received the blessings of The Holy Spirit. This mystical experience not only changed this book but also changed my life. This one gift transformed <u>Resurrecting Your Life</u> (originally titled <u>Don't Give Up, Get Up</u>) from 'just another inspirational/self-help book' to a spiritual tool that has blessed many people.

I have kept this story a secret for twenty years due to fear of criticism, but I know now is the perfect time to share it with the world.

The original cover of <u>Don't Give Up, Get Up</u> was going to be a sunrise to represent starting a new day of your life. As I designed the front cover I thought back to my younger years attending 'sunrise service' with my mother at Easter. I felt it was a perfect analogy for a book cover to display the concept of a new beginning and opportunity – my message in the book. Everything was perfectly planned for the publisher until I attended a church service at Camp Chesterfield in Chesterfield, Indiana.

On these sacred grounds in this little, quiet suburb of Anderson, Indiana there is a Spiritualist Church. For any of you who don't know, this is an organization/religion whose common denominator of thought is that loved ones who have passed can be contacted through mediums. I understand and accept that there will be some Christians who will stop reading my story at this time, outraged for going to such an 'evil' place. Yet they were drawn to the beautiful rendition of Jesus on the front cover, which I received the book while attending a service. But, on with the story…

Every Saturday night the church elders (called ministers/mediums) would do a demonstration of their God-given talents of contacting the 'other side." Some would do mediumship, some flame messages, and then there was this guy who was known to do 'spirit cards.' I had heard about him around the campus and had seen some of the cards that other people had received. They were beautiful with different original pictures on one side of the card and names of family members who had passed on the other side. While Ann and I desperately wanted to receive one of these cards for our own, I was still questioning if there was some kind of trick to this unbelievable demonstration.

It didn't take long to find out for myself. That night I watched the mystic walk on stage with a new package of blank, white index cards, still in the Walmart wrapper, and a small "snake" basket. Ann and I sat on the front row of pews in the tiny chapel. Another fifty people sat behind us all wanting the same thing – a card.

I didn't take my eyes off of the spiritual magician, trying to figure out his secret. He started by asking one of the audience members to open the pack of blank white cards and show everybody that all of them were blank. He then asked her to place the cards in the basket. Next, the medium added many types of markers – pens and pencils of different colors - then closed the basket. He didn't handle the basket. The basket was still sitting on the pulpit where he had originally placed it. He then informed us that he needed to meditate.

I watched as he went into a different consciousness. I didn't take my eyes off him. But to my surprise he didn't do anything except stand in the middle of the stage. He was not even close to the basket. After a short meditation he announced "they're done!" He quickly came out of his heightened state and started to open the basket. I felt an energy shoot through my body that I had never felt before. I told Ann, "the first card is for me." Somehow I just knew it!

As the medium pulled the first 'spirit card' from the basket he called my name. He said, "Jerry, this first card is for you. You are writing a book, aren't you?" I couldn't believe he knew about my book. Nobody knew I was just finishing my book. "This is for your front cover." When I heard him say it I didn't believe him because the plans for the front cover had been made, but the moment I saw the beautiful picture on the card I knew that the presses had to stop.

The rendition of Jesus on the front cover of this book is the original artwork that I first witnessed. The moment I put my eyes on the image I had Spirit chills run through my body. When I first showed the artwork to my publisher they questioned my rights to use it. They examined the brush strokes and lines under high power microscopes and decided that the art techniques used in the picture where very old and used by some of the masters. And the most amazing part of the puzzle is that this 'masterpiece' was manifested from a blank card in a closed basket in less than 15 minutes!

Was it real? We experienced something we can not explain or prove except for a picture – a special picture. The picture is real. The divine energy of the picture is real. This picture is a gift for you and every person who accepts the beauty and the love that it transmits.

Then the book was given a second gift – a truly miraculous happening. Receiving the first copy of <u>Resurrection</u> I was engrossed in reading every word on the back cover when my wife, Ann, walked up behind me and said, "oh, my God!" I quickly asked her what was wrong and she asked me to hand her the book. She slowly started pulling it farther away from me. As I stared at the back cover of the book the image appeared – there was a shadow of Jesus, very faint and 'behind' all the carefully crafted words that I had been so carefully scrutinizing. This second image of Jesus had not been planned.

The front and back cover design had been previously inspected and okayed by me. There was no such image on the proof of the book. But, here on the final back cover there was a faint image of Jesus. What was it and how did it get there?

I showed my publisher and asked him his professional opinion. He informed me it was a "burn-thru," which I guess means the ink somehow leaked onto the back page perfectly. I questioned the man who had printed many books, how many 'burn-thrus' he had seen. He couldn't remember the last one.

You can call it whatever you choose to call the obvious proof. There is an image of Jesus on the back cover. This image was not planned, So, please don't miss seeing it. I believe it was another gift from Spirit – that is The Holy Spirit to all of you who believe.

In The Beginning...

"In the beginning was the Word, and the Word was with God, and the word was God."

John 1:1-4

Presenting the prototype of this book to a few of my friends, I received one repeating comment - "that word 'God' bothers me. I think you should take it out, change it or write an explanation." Well, I knew I wasn't going to take it out and I didn't want to change it, so I took their third suggestion and decided to write this introduction.

I believe from my heart and soul that I never wrote these words to make anyone mad. But, the fact is this book might upset some people – the ones for whom these words go against their hardened beliefs. Yet, it could be the best thing that has ever happened to these blinded followers. The Bible sates "ye shall **know the truth** and the truth shall set you free." I would like to add: "but first, it might make you mad".

I'm not apologizing for using the word God or Jesus so many times in this book. It's a very important part of my life and true success. It's obvious why "God" and Jesus get eliminated from most business and self-help books; it is safer to eliminate these powerful, but risky, words so nobody is politically incorrect.

It reminds me of a program I presented. An attendee of my lecture congratulated me on how brave I was for presenting a spiritual class. The business owner explained how his staff had loved it, except for one of his employees, whom I made "really mad." I looked the man in the eyes and said "Good. Whoever I make mad is who I'm truly helping. I hit a nerve. That's good. It wakes them up.".

That's how I feel about this book. If the word God or Jesus offends you then maybe you should ask yourself *why* it offends you. Can you be truthful enough to ask yourself, and **listen to the truth**?

For most people, beliefs are difficult to change. Many of us have had toxic religious training – based on fear and guilt, shoved down our throats since childhood. Theologians claim that man's organized religion has pushed more people away from God than any other factor.

Contrary to how many of us have been taught, God is not a mean, hateful, vengeful person, watching over our every move. If you don't believe that, read I John in the Bible.

You can call God whatever you feel comfortable calling this divine energy. It is true that a name places a label on that which is impossible to label. This energy force that many of us call God, goes by many names. The name is not important. The concept of God is crucial.

Our Creator is all things. We are part of God. This divine energy is what created us, is part of us, and is always with us. God is not out there somewhere. S/He is with us every second of our lives. We don't have to worry if S/He hears us. The communication lines are always open.

We know we can **pray** to this superior being. We all believe this fact; but do you **believe that you can communicate with God**? You have the potential to **listen to God** when you **quiet your mind** and **listen to your inner voice.** As Scripture teaches, "Be still, and know that I am God." - Psalm 46:10

Religions have placed barriers separating God's children using dogmas and rituals. Yet, we are all saying the same words – God Is Love. Don't let your past beliefs, titles, or rituals stop you from experiencing <u>Resurrecting Your Life.</u>

Don't get hung up on trivial differences. This is the problem with mankind today – people look for the differences between human beings, instead of the similarities of their brothers and sisters of God.

I have chosen to **use the word "God"**. In I John it says that 'God is Love'. If you don't want to use the word "God", then **substitute Love in its place**.

The most important thing is to not allow the negative thought patterns of your past programming stop you from reading this book. If you don't **keep an open mind** and at least **read these words**, then you need this information the most.

I challenge you to **read <u>Resurrecting</u> <u>Your</u> <u>Life</u>** and then decide whether "our God" is your God. I absolutely know that once you **take the time to view these words,** you will agree that we are on the same team – God's.

From one who believes in the Positive Power of God, I welcome you. We have a mammoth mission and a tremendous responsibility of fighting for the good guys. Let's not quarrel among ourselves about trivial pursuits. Let all of us **lead by example** through loving each other – unconditionally. Let us not only talk about Jesus; let's **act like Him.**

This book is NOT a religious book. It is not necessarily a book only for Christians. Although I do feature Jesus, there are other enlightened ones who have walked on this earth to show us the divine way.

This book is NOT about Jesus. There are hundreds of volumes written about Him. What Resurrecting Your Life is, is a holistic health coaching manual using Jesus' teaching in our everyday lives. The truth is we have heard these spiritual words, and even repeated them but don't use them in our everyday life. Knowledge, known but never used, is the same as knowledge never known.

Jesus Christ never personally wrote a single book, was from the "wrong side of the tracks", never had a college education, never owned property, and was not known outside his immediate area. Yet, millions worship his name. Why? Because He had a God-given purpose and never lost the vision of His quest.

I believe He was sent not only to tell us the truth, but also to *show* us the truth. He is the perfect example and clearly leads us to a life of abundance. This is why He was so great and stated "Follow me.".

Even if you don't **believe in Jesus** the Savior, you cannot ignore the divine teachings that He shared – compassion, understanding, positive expectancy from divine guidance, honesty, and believing in a cause that was far greater than himself. If all of us could **live by these lessons**, the world would be a better place.

But most of all, Jesus showed us the miracle of resurrection, and promised each of us that we could do everything he did, and more. The act of rising from the dead is the ultimate example of what you can do today – right NOW! This act of faith was not something that only happened two thousand years ago. That great demonstration showed each of us that we must and can be born again; not just by words. We must roll the rock away. We must **take action**. We must **do something**.

Resurrecting Your Life gives you these spiritual teachings and proven path of action to **create your own personal miracle of rebirth** – starting over a new beginning. And all you have to do is **believe enough** to **have the faith** to **take action** and **begin your path of a new life!**

"But in fact, Christ has been raised from the dead, the first fruits of those who have fallen asleep. For as by a man came death, by a man has come also the resurrection of the dead. For as in Adam all die, so also in Christ shall all be made alive."

                                                                    I Corinthians 15:20

The Awakening

*"Don't part with your illusions. When they are gone you still exist, but you have ceased to **live**."*

Mark Twain

Resurrection – the miracle of rising from the dead. The Christian world is reminded each year how Jesus was resurrected from the grave. But this book is not about the miracle of Him coming back to life. Instead, these words have been written for every human being who has died at heart, is still walking and breathing, but is living a life of death.

Have you ever held onto a dream, only for it to wither and die? Have you experienced failure after failure, until you accepted the "obvious" conclusion – you *were* a failure? Are you discouraged or disappointed with your present state of living? Are you tired of being tired or sick of being sick? If any of these conditions describe you, then I have great news – the message is you can **rise** and **live again!**

Resurrection means more than just awakening from death. It is understanding that at one time there was life, then death, then the miracle of rebirth. You must **realize that what you now call life is actually an illusion or perception** formed by your previous programming, which you have received since birth. Many of your beliefs and judgments have been influenced by the darkness of negativity, which will never allow you to fulfill your God-given purpose.

The act of resurrection is a moment-by-moment reawakening and balancing of not only the physical body, but the mental, emotional and spiritual nature within each of us. You will do this by regaining energy, insight and awareness in all eight areas of your life. In this process of resurrecting yourself, you will **discover your God-given purpose** – why you are on this earth. It involves taking your life back in a positive way and living the life that your Creator intended for you to **live** and **enjoy** – the Positive Power of God.

This book had its own resurrection. While attending one of our classes, our teacher told me I had a great book, but the original title, Don't Give Up, Get Up, was not the correct title. She informed me that it should have no more than three words, and fewer was better. Since the book was in the final editing stages, I started to balk, but instead I listened to her advice. I had to admit, however painful it might be, that she was right. When my wife agreed with the teacher's opinion, I knew it had to be changed – but to what? It felt like I was changing one of my children's names.

Driving home from class, still questioning what the new title would be, a John Mellencamp song came on the radio. My ear caught some words in the song that I had heard many times before, but that night they were placed there for us to hear. Since we believe that everything happens for a purpose, my wife and I understood the significance of these words. The singer reminded us "life goes on, after the thrill of living is gone".

Ann broke the silence. "Resurrection. It just came to me. That's it – Resurrection."

The book now had new life, a tremendous title, and unlimited hope. It had been resurrected. It had changed, and so can you. All it takes from you is open-mindedness, faith and action. It is your choice to change or not to **change your life**, just like me changing the title. I could have left the original title. It would have been easier and safer. But now, looking back, I am thankful to God I changed it. You will be happy you had the desire and courage to change. It might not be easy, but when you look back, like I did, you'll be glad you had the courage to change. You can live again if you truly **desire a new life** and **believe in the Positive Power of God.**

****

I was listening to a story that was told to me by a religious woman. It was about a resurrection. A plumber, who was a God-fearing man, had a good friend who had just passed away, and had been taken to the coroner. As he was grieving for his deceased friend, he was asked by God why he was mourning. "Your friend is not dead. He is only sleeping. Go and awaken him with your belief in the name of Jesus." At first the man questioned himself. He thought his mind was playing tricks on him, but again he was told his mission. This time he believed the words were truly a message from God and went to perform this act of faith.

The man entered the room where his friend was lying, picked the body up in his arms, stood it against the wall and commanded: "Walk in the name of Jesus.". To no one's amazement, the body slumped to the floor. The man stood the lifeless body up again, and this time a little louder stated "Walk in the name of Jesus.". And again, the body fell to the floor. At this point, many of us would have given up, but not this determined friend. The plumber, not losing his faith, picked the body up once more and threw the limp man against the wall as he shouted at the top of his lungs: "Walk in the name of Jesus!" and the man came alive and walked! This one man, because of his faith and ability to act, had resurrected his friend. It was a miracle!

Is this story true? I don't honestly know because I wasn't there. The lady swore to me that it was true. And later I had another lady who confirmed the story. Yet, many of you will probably still not **believe** this story any more than you **believe in yourself and your abilities.** There are miracles happening every day. You are God's potential miracle just waiting to happen. Do you believe that you **possess unlimited power** that is just waiting to explode? Or do you believe that you are not worthy enough to perform such as wonderful miracle as resurrection? Oh, ye of little faith, **believe** and you will **move mountains!**

****

God has given each of us the power to **perform the miracle of resurrection.** And the first person you must restore life to is yourself.

Are you living or dead? Many of you will question the validity of such an inquiry. "Of course, I'm alive. I am breathing. My heart's beating. I'm moving. Sure, I'm living." And in a literal, physical sense you are correct. But what about your inner self – your soul? Is it still alive or has the divine spark been extinguished by the woes of daily living and stress?

Are you living or just existing? Are you thriving or only surviving? Many people are what I refer to as "the walking dead". They are sleepwalking through life. These sad souls, who really don't understand the truth, are wearing masks of success, happiness, and prosperity, concealing the real person, who is dying from the dis-eases of darkness, such as fear, guilt, jealousy, envy and lack of purpose.

Too many of these suffering people know deep down inside that there is something wrong, that there is more to do and experience; but they won't allow their souls to show them their true path of enlightenment. Instead, they believe that the way they are living is the only way to live.

They falsely believe they must suffer. They place their hope in false prophets. And all they have to do is believe in the Positive Power of God.

The real truth of the matter is that YOU have the choice to **perform the biggest miracle** in the world – resurrecting yourself. You don't have to be thrown against the wall, or die, in order to be brought back to life (although some people might have to go to those extremes).

Each and every one of you is designed for success and destined for greatness; yet so many bathe in the pity of negativity. It is not God's fault. It is not society's fault. It is nobody's fault but your own if you are not where you want to be. God gave every human being two gifts that He did not give to any of His other creations – the power of imagination, and willpower.

To **create this miracle of a new life,** you must first **decide you want to live again.** You must **make the choice** that you are tired of how you are experiencing life and you want to **change.** To do this, you must **eliminate your negative thinking** and **accept the Positive Power of God.** You always have the choice of how you **think.** Choosing to **live the positive way** of God is absolutely crucial in resurrecting your life.

The next step is to **use your imagination** and **dream** about the perfect life in which you can help spread God's Great News. It's that simple – maybe not easy, but simple.

Resurrection is a revival of the soul's purpose. Many people are going through the motions of living, but their heart and soul have died. Henry David Thoreau stated it perfectly when he wrote: "most men lead lives of quiet desperation and go to the grave with their song still in them". These unfortunate sleepwalkers don't realize they have died, yet they must admit they don't have the same energy and passion for life they once possessed. What happened?

Let's examine the word 'revive'. The definition states "to **give new life**". Is this not what many of us need and desire – a new beginning, a fresh start? Synonyms of revive are renewal; restoration; refreshment; improvement; awakening; and rebirth. And there is one place to **find all of these things** and more – with the Positive Power of God.

Picture a man who is dying, who needs emergency medical attention. He is lying there, fighting for his life.

He has lost consciousness, movement, and energy flow. The medical experts work hard on reviving him. If they are successful, he regains energy, movement, and life. If they are unsuccessful, the patient loses his energy source, his heart stops, he dies, and his soul leaves. Death is a loss of energy, much like a car battery that has lost its charge. Without energy, the body can no longer function. Without a purpose, the soul's passion withers and that person complains "I'm tired".

How do you **know** if you need to be revived? **Ask yourself if you have the energy and passion that you once enjoyed.** Many people falsely believe they have lost their energy because of reaching a certain age, but this is only an excuse. There are many seventy-year-olds who have an enormous amount of energy and life. All of us know some sixteen-year-olds who complain they have no energy. So, age is not the reason why a person suffers from a lack of energy. So, if it is not age, what is it?

A lady recently visited me and after a few minutes of friendly chat she confessed to me that she had no energy. The woman was only forty years old so I was positive it was not caused by her age. She seemed healthy. I asked her permission to ask a few personal questions. Immediately, I realized the problem – she was a member of "the walking dead". She was negative on herself, life, job, husband and family. She was hurting, and I knew she had two choices – to be resurrected or die a long, frustrating death. It was her choice, just like it is your choice and mine.

This unhappy lady had lost the most precious gift that God gives each and every one of us – the gift of life. She had substituted anger, fear and frustration for joy, love and thankfulness. She didn't have to die to go to hell. She was living in hell every day of her life.

Many people exist in a living hell every day because of something they have done in their past. These people have acted as judge and jury against themselves and continue punishing themselves daily. Much like the lady in the story above, they have allowed their past failures and disappointments to make their life a living hell. This is the reason so many people are unhappy, negative, and bitter. They have lost hope of living the life they had once dreamed, so instead of feeling the hurt, they choose to die an emotional death of lies, conceit and low self-esteem.

They live in the darkness. They do not understand that God loves them no matter what they have done.

To **rejuvenate yourself**, you must **understand** that now is the only time there is. The past is gone, and tomorrow is always ahead of you. The only thing you have that you can control by the choices you make is today – right now. Today is a gift from God, and that is why it is called "the present". Cherish it. Use it to **achieve your God-given dreams.**

It is so easy to **state the words** that all of us have the choice to live in our own heaven or hell every day that we inhabit this Earth. Yet, most of us have to confess it is much easier said than done. But, I do promise you there is **hope.** There is a better way to live. You can **live in heaven** every day. You don't have to suffer. And all you have to do is **have the desire to change** the lifestyle you are experiencing now and **have faith in God** and **believe** that He will help you **resurrect your life.** You can **perform a miracle** if you only take the first steps – **have faith in God,** and in yourself, and **have the courage to do something** about it.

"I am resurrection and the life; he that believeth in me, though he were dead, yet shall he live. And whosoever liveth and believeth in me shall never die. Believeth thou this?"

John 11:2

Love Is The Answer

"He that loveth not his brother, abideth in death."

I John 3:14

For centuries we have been taught the answer to all of our problems, yet we have not listened or learned. The message was too simple – love is the answer. This four-letter word is so misunderstood, misused and taken for granted that many people don't **understand the power** in such a tiny word. Yet, **take the time to evaluate the word 'love'**, and it will show you the secret of reviving yourself.

We have all heard the familiar phrase – God is love. But, what does that mean? It is imperative to **understand the full meaning of love** to truly **know who and what is God.** I Corinthians 13: 4-8 states "Love is patient and kind. Love is not jealous, it does not brag, and it is not proud. Love is not rude, is not selfish and does not get upset with others. Love does not count up wrongs that have been done. Love is not happy with evil but is happy with the truth. Love patiently accepts all things. It always trusts, always hopes and always remains strong. Love never fails". Where there is love, there is God, and where there is God, there is love.

As human beings we can be controlled by our emotions. And all emotions originate from either a thought of love or fear. Love is always a positive thought, while fear is a negative vibration. For every thought, word, there is a response or reaction. A positive thought results in a response. A negative thought creates a reaction.

The concept of love is best explained by the ancient Greeks. Because of the complexity of the word "love", they developed four different definitions for it. *Eros* is romantic love, while *Storge* is love for our family and security. *Phileo* is the type of love we feel for our friends. However, the most important type of love is *Agape* – the unselfish love, which expects nothing in return. This is the love that Jesus lived and taught. This is the love that each of us should **strive to experience** throughout our lives.

Agape is the unconditional love God gives you, no matter what you've done or not done; have or don't have. And this type of forgiving love is how He wants all of us to live. Love is a verb as well as a noun. It takes time, practice and patience, but you can learn how to "do love"

\gape throughout your life. It can become ıthing. Agape is a choice that you make, happens or how you personally feel.

To better **understand the concept of love, ask yourself the question 'why'** you are thinking a certain thought, saying particular words, or performing a specific action. If you **ask** enough 'why's, the path will lead to your first thought, which was based from either love or fear.

If your answer is hate, jealousy, frustration, envy, or guilt, know that these are all forms of fear. Fear is the opposite of love. Perfect love casts out all fear. And since God is perfect love, then when we choose negative emotions we are not trusting God (love), which is a sin.

An acronym of fear is <u>F</u>alse <u>E</u>xpectations <u>A</u>ppearing <u>R</u>eal. When we feel these negative vibrations, we are picturing images in our mind, to which we react and 'cop an attitude'. When we picture the dark side, we are not in tune or on the same frequency of the Positive Power of God. Worry and anxiety are clear examples of lack of love. These "mind viruses" keep you away from God (love).

Negative energy is never divinely enhanced. Negativity will never **make your life better** or help you **discover** and always remains strong. Love never fails". Where there is love, there is God, and where there is God, there is love."

As human beings we can be controlled by our emotions. And all emotions originate from either a thought of love or fear. Love is always a positive thought, while fear is a negative vibration. For every thought, word, there is a response or reaction. A positive thought results in a response. A negative thought creates a reaction.

The concept of love is best explained by the ancient Greeks. Because of the complexity of the word "love", they developed four different definitions for it. *Eros* is romantic love, while *Storge* is love for our family and security. *Phileo* is the type of love we feel for our friends. However, the most important type of love is *Agape* – the unselfish love, which expects nothing in return. This is the love that Jesus lived and taught. This is the love that each of us should **strive to experience** throughout our lives.

Agape is the unconditional love God gives you, no matter what you've done or not done; have or don't have. And this type of forgiving love is how He wants all of us to live. Love is a verb as well as a noun. It takes time, practice and patience, but you can learn how to "do love" and experience Agape throughout your life. It can become as natural as breathing. Agape is a choice that you make, regardless of what happens or how you personally feel.

To better **understand the concept of love, ask yourself the question 'why'** you are thinking a certain thought, saying particular words, or performing a specific action. If you **ask** enough 'why's, the path will lead to your first thought, which was based from either love or fear.

If your answer is hate, jealousy, frustration, envy, or guilt, know that these are all forms of fear. Fear is the opposite of love. Perfect love casts out all fear. And since God is perfect love, then when we choose negative emotions we are not trusting God (love), which is a sin.

An acronym of fear is False Expectations Appearing Real. When we feel these negative vibrations, we are picturing images in our mind, to which we react and 'cop an attitude'. When we picture the dark side, we are not in tune or on the same frequency of the Positive Power of God. Worry and anxiety are clear examples of lack of love. These "mind viruses" keep you away from God (love).

Negative energy is never divinely enhanced. Negativity will never **make your life better** or help you **discover**

your true purpose. God's message – and He has one for every problem you are facing – is always positive. If it's not loving, positive words that uplift you, then it is not from the ultimate, divine energy that many of us call God.

God is love. God is pure positive energy. Jesus, his son, whom He sent to Earth to show us the way, was always positive. His God-given purpose for which He gave His life was to show us how to live in the light of love. Love is a positive energy. Wherever there is love there is Light, and where there is Light, there is love. The power of love can move mountains. Joy, kindness and gratitude are the building blocks that will help you **build your new life.** Discover the "attitude of gratitude".

To **find this special love,** you must **eliminate your negativity.**

The best way to do this is to **focus on what you have,** not what you don't have. You don't have to look far to find people who would love to have your life. Don't take such a precious thing for granted. Wherever you are at this time in your life, you are there because of your emotions (love or fear), what you believe, your thinking (positive or negative), words and actions. It is not God's fault. It isn't your parent's fault. There is only one person you can point the finger at – yourself.

You and God, working together, can **perform this miracle** of a new life. Ask yourself the should-searching questions – Are you where you want to be in life? Are you who you want to be? Do you **know Jesus?** Are you doing what He wants you to do; giving what He wants you to give; feeling the way you want to feel? If you aren't doing what you feel God wants you to do, there is no doubt that fear has conquered you.

If you **have the courage to admit** that you are not living the life God desires; are open-minded to a better way of living, and are ready to **eliminate your negative thinking,** then you are ready to **live the great life** that God has planned for you. You are ready for the day that you've been waiting for and dreaming about – your day of resurrection. Today begins the rest of your life. **Live it with enthusiasm** by using the power of God that is within each and every human being. No matter what you have done or not done in your past, this power is within you, just waiting to be awakened.

The first step in learning how to **use this positive energy of love** as a weapon against the forces of negativity is finding the faith to **believe in God.** Faith is the substance of things hoped for, believing that they will manifest, although not seen yet (Hebrews 11:1). You must **have faith and believe that God loves you**, no matter what you've done. This is called unconditional love – Agape.

Since your Father/God forgives you, then you should be able to **forgive yourself** and **quit beating yourself up** for yesterday's mistakes that you have no control over. Rejoice! **Be positive. Be God-like.** Follow in the steps of the great master. **Let love flow** through you and around you. Follow God's example of unconditional love. As Ann and I were driving to a weekend retreat, we passed a billboard on the side of the interstate. The big white sign stood almost bare, except for the few bold, black words that clearly conveyed the message: I said 'Love thy neighbor, and I'm not kidding' – it was signed GOD.

God is calling you. He needs your help, and you need Him. He promises to love you through thick and thin, and all He wants back is for you to **show your love** for Him. The way that you show your love is to **love your**

neighbor – every person that gets within three feet of you every minute of every hour. And all you have to do is **smile!**

That's right, just **smile at every person** you meet tomorrow. **Don't worry,** there's no cost to these smiles and you can't run empty. As a matter of fact, you can go miles with smiles. You never know, you might even get some back in return. Whether you do or don't, I guarantee you that you will be on the first step of resurrecting yourself by showing God that you **thank Him** for His love and just **keep returning that love.** Through love you will **find the Positive Power of God.**

The second step of rebirth is loving yourself – **be positive** about yourself. You achieve this task much like the first demonstration, with one major difference; this time you **express God's love** inwardly to yourself. Smile to yourself. **Watch yourself** in a mirror. **Have fun. Loosen up.** Too many of you are the hardest task masters on yourself. You wouldn't put up with it from someone else. Why do you accept the abuse from yourself?

If you truly want to **know God** and **love God,** then you have to **love yourself** because God is all, and all is God.

Which means that if you don't love yourself, then you are not loving God.

The reason that most people don't like themselves is negative thought patterns. These established programs dictate how you perceive the world. If you have had negative input throughout your life, it will be difficult to see the light. Until you rid yourself of disempowering beliefs, you will suffer. These thoughts of darkness are blocking your soul from the light of positive energy – Jesus the Christ.

When a negative thought flashes into your mind you must immediately **find the positive** in the same thought. This technique is known as reframing. Remember, God gave all of us the ability to choose. He won't ever dictate your fate. You have the choice of how you perceive every situation. A happening is not necessarily positive or negative, or good or bad. It just is. It is exactly what you **choose** to frame it. By choosing the positive view of the event, you are choosing God and love.

The next step of loving yourself is finding what you like about yourself, not what you don't like. Catch yourself doing something "right" instead of wrong. **Laugh with yourself. Admit your mistakes** (and **remember, there**

is no such thing as a mistake if you **reframe it into a positive lesson**).

A wonderful exercise is to **invest fifteen seconds every day and make yourself laugh.** I know it sounds silly, but laughter is the best medicine. It might feel stupid the first time but **do it** anyway. Once you start, you can't stop. It does **feel good**.

The third and final part of your journey is to repeat this last exercise with all of your "neighbors". Find out what you like about every person you meet, smile (exercise 1) and **give them a sincere compliment. Catch them doing something right** and **tell them** so. **Share with them a positive word**. If you're really good, try to get eye contact. Remember, the eyes are the windows of the soul.

Some of you will **read** through these seemingly simple steps and not see the power of these actions. I only ask you to **execute the plan** and **see for yourself.** Some will laugh and ridicule. People laugh because they don't understand and are not courageous enough to ask. **Forgive** them because they don't **understand**. The words of Jesus Christ are simple – **Love God with all your heart** and all your mind and all your soul. **Treat yourself as if your body is the temple of God. Love thy neighbor**.

Start these three exercises:

1. **Share a smile with everybody.**
2. **Compliment yourself. Catch yourself doing something right.**
3. **Love thy neighbor. Find the positive about each person.**

What the world needs now is love – God. All of us can **use more love** in our lives – more positive energy. The world is a negative place. All of us get beat down in our daily challenges. But the light of Jesus Christ will give you the strength you need to **resurrect your life** into a more meaningful purpose. The more love you give as you start your **walk with Jesus,** the more positive vibrations you will experience. This starts eliminating a moment of darkness. You will **see the light** if you **continue the challenge.** The question is; will you **accept the challenge of the quest**?

"Beloved, let us love one another; for love is of God' and every one that loveth is born of God and knoweth God. He that loveth not, knoweth not God, for God is love."

1 John 4: 7-8

The Challenge

"I can do all things through Christ which strengtheneth me"

Phil. 4:13

Do you **dream about things** you would like to do or have; places you would like to go; or a certain amount of money you would like to earn? Do you **feel that God has revealed His plans for your life** or are you, like many people, floundering in the struggle of daily living, just trying to get by? To **be resurrected from the living dead** you must **have a God-given dream** and **believe that God will help you** achieve this vision. The Bible states that without a vision the people will perish. No truer words have ever been written. You must **have a reason to live and love.** It doesn't matter whether it is a large or small dream. But to **live life to the ultimate** you must **have a purpose** that you passionately believe in; that wakes you up every morning and instills the power of purpose in you.

God gives all of us a unique dream. Nobody argues that they have never dreamed. Where do these dreams come from? God gives us the ability to **imagine into the future.**

A few of us are living out this constant thought and idea process in our head; some are still chasing their dream; but many have lost the sight of their dreams, blinded by the daily stress, frustration and reality of everyday survival.

A person who has forfeited his/her dreams is a sad sight. This person has lost the zest for life. They have forgotten that all of us are created in the image of God, and He is a creator - not a quitter. They do not **understand the words of Jesus Christ.** The spark of Godliness deep inside them is sleeping (they have literally 'sold their soul'). They have submitted to the darkness of negativity, accepting what society gives them instead of facing the truth and claiming what they rightfully deserve – abundance and peace of mind.

So many people are sleepwalking through the daily grind, putting their life into a job for one purpose – a paycheck. The truth is that money buys things, but never quiets the desperation of the soul. Feelings such as depression, negativity, anger and bitterness are a few of the signs the soul uses to warn us that we are off track. Our answer is to kill the messenger with drugs and other addictions, all designed for one purpose – to eliminate the pain. This is the same pain that is trying to save our souls.

This is not the way that God intended His greatest miracles to spend their time on Earth. Yet, as creatures of negative thinking they have lost their faith in not only God, but in themselves. They don't know the truth! They have been exposed to the deadly dis-ease of negativism and live their lives in fear and darkness. They meet each day with an ugly attitude about a life that holds more riches than they could ever humanly imagine.

AMERICA NEEDS AN ATTITUDE ADJUSTMENT!!! We are the 'richest' country in the world, yet our society is in a mess. Lives and families are being sacrificed for the so-called "pursuit of happiness". Men and women are dying everyday with their song still in their heart.

We are currently experiencing the largest epidemic in the history of mankind. It is more widespread than heart disease, cancer and AIDS combined. It is a silent killer, and there is no pill, shot or transplant that can help. This dis-ease starts as closed-mindedness. In this early stage of development, the afflicted one chooses to no longer take in new ideas. S/He shuts down the oxygen flow of new thoughts. From this lack of freshness, the mind starts to rot and advances into Stinking Thinking. This condition can be detected by a negative personality and bad attitude. Every time the person speaks, the words are negative garbage, such as gossip, cursing, complaining and backstabbing. This stage is worse than bad breath, because you don't have to listen to bad breath all day.

Once stinking thinking has set in, the Hardening of the Attitudes appear. At this level of the dis-ease, the victim's attitude is not only negative, but s/he absolutely refuses to change his or her way of thinking or living. This quickly produces the advanced stage of deterioration – Analysis Paralysis. This condition of imagined fear and negativity prevents the afflicted from taking any action. No action, no goals, no results, no change, makes for a boring, unfulfilled life – death. At this time the victim is pronounced as one of the Walking Dead.

Does this sound like somebody you might know? Someone fairly close? Do you see yourself in one of these stages of this terrible plague? This epidemic is called Negativism (Can't-itis). Beware, this virus is highly contagious and deadly to your future. But, don't worry. There is hope. It's called The Positive Power of God!

To **awaken yourself** and **receive what is rightfully yours**, you must **have the "right thinking"**. This positive state of mind is what Jesus referred to as "righteousness or Christ consciousness". You must positively **know that you can do, be, have and give more**. But you must be careful, because every day you will be confronted by negative forces that will try to stop you from being all you can be. With the Positive Power of God, you can **defeat the negative forces** and **win at the game of life**. The Force of God is truly with you.

It is your God-given right to be successful. But, before you can be successful, you must **understand what success really is**. The illusion of success is different to each of us. To attain success, you must **know what it personally means to you**. It makes no difference what I, or anyone else, believes that success is.

Ralph Waldo Emerson eloquently described success - "to **laugh often** and much; to **win the respect of intelligent people** and the affection of children; to **earn the appreciation of honest critics** and **endure the betrayal** of **false friends**; to **appreciate beauty, to find the best in others;** to **leave the world a bit better**, whether by a healthy child, a garden patch, **or** a redeemed social condition; to **know even one life has breathed easier because you have lived**. This is to have succeeded."

Success to me is living my life the way that God has planned for me. If I do my very best toward the goals that God and I have set together; if I smile, **compliment others** and **pass on God's unconditional love** today, then I have been a great success in my eyes and in His.

To **partake in this earthly feast** of success and abundance, you must **learn what God has planned for you.** He needs messengers in all phases of work and every economic level. You need to **establish a relationship with your God. Start by believing in Jesus Christ**. You cannot afford to be struck down by this deadly dis-ease of negativity. Performing the miracle of resurrection takes a strong desire to **live again** and having faith in yourself and God that you can **accomplish your dreams.** If you **possess these traits** you will **rise to the top** and **live the life you have always dreamed.**

Resurrecting Your Life can help you **find God as a partner in Life; rejoin the living**; **have more energy** and enthusiasm; **achieve your dreams** and **discover your life purpose,** no matter what level of life you are experiencing at this time. Whether you are down and depressed, feeling lost on your journey of life, or just asking "now what?", these words will help you **recreate the positive attitude,** burning desire and success that God wants to see you achieve.

God has given you everything you need for success inside you. The only thing that is stopping you is you. **Don't let anybody tell you that you can't** – especially that critical voice inside your head. **Don't allow anything to stop you**. God is on your side and that's always the winning team!

Are you ready to **live life to its fullest** and **experience the life that God planned for you?** If you are, then it's time to **take your life back. Have the courage to take the first step. Don't let fear stop you**. If you **tell yourself that nothing will stop you,** then nothing will. With God on your side, no one can prevail against you. The Positive Power of God's love is with you every second of every day. He will never desert you, and that's a promise from God!

I challenge you to **change <u>your</u> world.** I challenge you to **change**. It won't be easy. The beginning of anything worthwhile is never easy. But, who promised you life was going to be easy? It is simple to follow the beaten down path that you are now traveling, but is that where you want to be? If you don't like who you are at this moment, you must **change something.** To **transform your life** you must **take positive action** and **start this moment with a positive thought.**

God has given you the power to **change whatever you don't like** that is happening in your life. One of the goals of life should be to **be happy.** Whatever you're not happy about in your life, change it – NOW! But, it is up to you. Nobody else can motivate you to **transform your life**. Nobody else can resurrect you. You must **do it** yourself. Only you have the key that opens the door to greatness and true happiness. It's always your choice. **Choose it wisely.**

I understand the feeling that Patrick Henry must have felt when he bellowed "Give me liberty or give me death!". I also feel the sadness he must have felt when his words were heard by many but few listened, and fewer responded.

I thank God that I am allowed to **share this information** with you. I am crying the words of freedom to all of you. **Arm yourself against the tyranny of fear,** which keeps you oppressed and **take back your most precious possession** – your life. Many of us live in a self-imposed prison of our own negativity. The ironic part of life is that YOU hold the key to **free yourself.** All you have to do is have the courage to **use the key.** Do you **have the courage?**

I understand that only a few of you will **take the time to read** or **listen to these words**, although many will have the opportunity to **partake**. I know that even less will use what they have learned and combine it with belief to **take action**. Will you **be one of the few** who are enlightened enough to **cherish this opportunity** and **discover the Positive Power of God** in these words?

I pray that if you are not completely satisfied with your life, you will allow me the opportunity to share what I know is the truth – the words of Jesus Christ. Ann and I attempt to model our lives from our teacher – Jesus. We are wagering our lives on these God-given concepts you are now holding in your hands. These teachings, which are supported by Bible scripture, saved us and they can save you. We were able to restore our faith in Jesus Christ and **learn how to use the power of The Holy Spirit.** You can too; all you have to do is **open your heart** and **absorb these words into your soul** with an open mind.

Who was Jesus? How did this one poor, lone Galilean preacher and teacher turn the world upside down? What did He offer that was so different? There is no doubt that Jesus was a revolutionary teacher. He is easily one of the most important figures in the history of mankind. Yet, He did not teach a word of theology. Even more surprising is that He did not write down His teachings. But, why are His teachings so important for you to be able to **resurrect yourself?**

This messenger from God taught a new way for mankind to live. He promised love, happiness, health, peace of mind and abundance. His message is the Truth. It is the answer that eliminates evil and transforms our lives into the best we can be. Jesus still makes this offer to each of us today. With that kind of promise, how could any of us go wrong?

Jesus was sent to this Earth for a purpose – just like you and me. He had a challenge – a quest. He understood the importance of His mission. Jesus did not falter from his divine path, even when his own family thought he was strange or his life was in jeopardy. How much are you willing to risk to **follow your God-inspired dreams**?

It will be difficult at first to **accept these new beliefs.** It will be easier to hold onto your old habits, not giving the new information a chance and fabricating an excuse why you can't. But, before you rush into a decision, **listen to that little voice** deep inside you. It never lies. This quiet voice is your hotline to the ultimate intelligence of God. If you need this program, it will tell you. The real question is; will you **be quiet** long enough to **listen** and **trust your inner guidance system**, or will you block your feelings like so many people?

The teaching of Jesus Christ is for people who are ready to **change** – who want to **make a difference**. There is no reason to try to "sell" this idea to you. It is not a commodity that will go bad or out of fashion. You will thirst for these words when the time is right. These words were true two thousand years ago, are valid today, and will be essential a hundred years into the future. Are you prepared and advanced enough in your life to **learn these lessons**? Remember, when the student is ready the teacher will appear. Are you ready to **accept the challenge** to **discover your quest** and **live this quest with passion?**

All you have to have is the courage to **take the next step.** Don't let fear or negativity rob you of your birthright. You have been designed for success and are destined for greatness. God didn't make any failures, and you are one of God's creations. **Don't delay. Make the decision today. Bring the Positive Power of God into your life** and **live it with enthusiasm**.

Turn the page. **Take that famous first step on a magnificent journey of recreation**. A thousand-mile journey starts with a single step. And even after only one small step, you are closer to living the life that you've always dreamed of living. Congratulations for making the best decision in your life and accepting the challenge of fulfilling your God-given quest.

As we have opportunity, **let us do good (God)** unto all men....

Galatians 6:10

I Have A Dream... Do You?

"Where there is no vision, the people perish"

Proverbs.29:18

For you to **get started on your journey of re-creation** you must first **invest some time** and **do a process called "re-minding"**. To "re-mind" is to **bring back the mind that you once had** before your dreams died – before they were taken away from you. Do you **remember a time in your life when you had passion** and felt wonderful about yourself? **Return to those glory days in your** mind when you dreamed visions that you believed would really come true.

Take a few moments and reflect. Find that special moment when you had that burning desire to achieve something and be somebody. Once you **allow your mind to reminisce** back to those happy days, **notice how you feel.** If you have truly traveled back in time, your body has changed; your breathing is different, you **feel more confident** and enthusiastic about life. This is no accident. By going back and reliving accomplishments in your life, you are able to locate a time that you were on your God-given path. At this moment, you felt great because you were living the true you. If just a memory can bring back such positive feelings, can you **imagine how living life like that again would feel**?

I held onto several of my visions for many years, and every day I inched closer to their reality. I have faith that if I do everything I can possibly do to achieve my dreams, then God will lend me a hand. I have seen many of my visions become reality including this book. I also have more visions that I will continue working toward every step of the day. The most important thing is never not have a vision you are striving for.

I have been involved in motivation – believing in the positive way of living, for over twenty-five years. I wasn't born positive or raised in a positive home, but I am positive now. I have always believed in God, but I did not understand the positive impact God was going to make in my life.

Am I always positive? No. I have my bad days just like every other human being on this planet. The only perfect human being who has ever walked on earth has been Jesus Christ. All of us need to walk in His shoes and then we would understand how to live a Christ-conscious life. Through His words and examples, we can **learn how to improve our lives** and get closer to living our God-given potential. He will take our hand and teach us how to **make every day a beautiful day.**

The difference of how positive and negative people cope with the challenges of everyday living is a crucial secret of true happiness and success. You must be more than a reborn Christian. You must **learn, accept** and **discipline yourself** to what God wants to do with your life, and **do it in a positive, loving way.** This is one secret you will want to learn and live by as you **travel on your journey of enlightenment**.

Everything happens for a purpose on your daily travels. It is much easier to **be positive** and **use the Positive Power of** God when you **trust that every experience is a learning lesson. Don't hate** what happens to you. Don't look at it as a negative. **Use the experience** by asking yourself, "how can I learn from this?" Whatever happens to you that doesn't kill you, will make you stronger. I guarantee that, and we are living proof of it.

When God first placed the concept of motivation and positive thinking in my head, people laughed at my new thinking. But I didn't allow their comments to stop me as I studied and attempted to **live by the positive words.** There will be people who will make fun of you as you work on remembering your God-given dreams and **advance in your lessons.** It was like my own religion. It didn't matter what others thought or said. I was so motivated and positive, my energy and enthusiasm won people over to my side. And this, too, will happen to you. Don't let others influence your thinking as your life changes. You and only you **understand** and **know what the right path is to travel on your personal journey.**

One of the first benefits of living with the Positive Power of God is the amount of enthusiasm and energy you receive. The word "enthusiasm" is derived from a Greek word that means, "God or spirit within". An acronym for the 'iasm' of enthusiasm is "I Am Sold Myself". When you **become excited** about who you are becoming, not in an egotistical way, but in a confident, positive manner, you will **live your life with Positive Power.** When you **have a relationship with God,** this secret energy will be bestowed upon you.

You will **see the world in a totally new light**. You will **have the fire and the magic that attracts true success** and happiness like a magnet.

At one time, I wanted to be materially successful, as do most of us. I had an ego-based vision. I longed for money and success, and I achieved it. The problem was I had paid a high price. The real riches of life – a loving family, good health, and peace-of- mind were not in my agenda at this time.

The books of the motivational gurus promised to show me a way to live my life to the fullest, build my self-esteem and live the dreams that I never thought possible. I can still remember writing down my first list of goals. Ann, my wife, and I were living in the upstairs of an old apartment house. I was studying on the enclosed deck of the small three-room (not three bedroom) apartment. Here we sat with no jobs. Our van had been repossessed; we had no money and I was just starting a new career as a hairdresser.

I sat at the small table and wrote down such outrageous statements as owning our own home within five years, working as an educator for a national company in the hairdressing business, and having two children. The written down goal actually described our first child as 'our first child is a girl. Her name is Leslie. She is petite and feminine. Our second child is a boy.' Our first child *was* a girl. Her name *is* Leslie and the description fits her perfectly. Our second child *was* a boy and we named him Michael.

This part of the story might not sound too exciting until you understand that Ann, who had been married before, was told by various doctors that she would <u>never</u> have children. She had spent thousands of dollars to have children, all in vain. Our dream was for her to birth Leslie before she was thirty years old. Leslie was born on July 1, 1979, which made Ann 29 ½ years old! The combination of the Positive Power of God and goal-setting created a miracle!

The freedom to dream is crucial for goal setting. It's a process that you not only should **learn to master**, but also **make part of your daily ritual**. I now know that because of the Positive Power of God and doing the goal-setting exercise, every one of my original goals was accomplished. I wasn't sure at first if the process of goal-setting would work. But I had nothing to lose and everything to gain, so I responded through faith in the information I had learned and took action. Isn't this exactly what many of you should do?

Today, I can honestly say that I have never not achieved a goal that God and I properly wrote down and followed through the steps that are described in this book! The Positive Power of God works, and it will help you **perform the miracle of resurrection** and **manifest those dreams** that you are so desperately searching for.

Our accomplishments were many, but there was trouble coming. We didn't have the Holy Spirit guiding and protecting us. As successful as it seemed we were, the truth was that we were not happy. Our lifestyle became more stressful every day until our health started failing. The realization of truth hit me when I saw my wife wearing a heart monitor. Our family doctor warned her if she didn't change, the stress would kill her. Our family started falling apart; the business was failing, we lost our lease, our employees walked out, and the I.R.S. audited us.

My vision – notice I say "my" vision, instead of "God's and my vision" quickly became a living nightmare for my wife, children and me. We plummeted from the high life to the brink of bankruptcy before we knew what had really happened. Even today, looking back on the experience, we ask ourselves "what in the world happened?". We went from having everything to having nothing. We had lost twenty years of work. It was devastating. It was humbling. At the lowest ebb of my life I did something I hadn't done since I was a child. I prayed to God.

I had studied motivation for twenty-five years, so I knew I was motivated. I knew how to **set goals** and **think positive**, but there was still something not quite right. Why weren't our lives working out? That missing ingredient was a relationship with Jesus Christ.

At one of the lowest times in our journey, Ann and I decided to go to church. We didn't know where to go so each Sunday we visited a different church to find the right one. One Sunday, a minister friend of mine asked me if I had the Holy Spirit. I had no idea what he was talking about, but he intrigued me enough that Ann and I started going there every week.

The longer we attended, the more interested I became. I realized that everything I had been studying in motivation related to religion. I was hooked. I had a new vision. I dreamed of sharing my information in a new way – this time God and we were partners. I received a vision of teaching the Positive Power of God through the words of Jesus Christ.

I shared my new vision with the pastor. He listened silently to my enthusiastic pitch of what I wanted to do. As I took a breath, he interrupted, "what is your relationship with Jesus Christ?"

I was shocked by the question and answered "I've been baptized".

He rebuked "you're going to need more than that if you want to **accomplish your dream**".

Pastor Charles had me hook, line and sinker and now he was reeling me in. "What more do I need?" I asked.

"You need the Holy Spirit."

"What's that and how do I get it?" I was ready to do almost anything to get myself and my family out of hardship. The pastor gave me some literature, told me to read it, and he would see us Sunday.

The next Sunday a new feeling came over both Ann and me. Both of us repented our sins, surrendered our lives to Jesus Christ, and received the Holy Spirit. Our lives and our vision have never been the same since.

****

Do you ever feel like you aren't doing what you really want to do? Have your dreams or visions been stolen from you or put on the shelf as you struggle with family responsibilities? It's natural to feel this way. Every successful person has felt this way at one time or another. I now refer to this as "Divine Discontent". You must **trust your feelings**. The reason I call this "Divine Discontent" is that when you **feel this restlessness inside** yourself, God is telling you that you are not on the true path He has planned for you. By remembering your dreams and passion, you will be closer to your Creator. This new relationship will set you free, and you will have **peace of mind.**

The Bible states "Where there is no vision, people perish" (Proverbs 29:18). This clearly confirms the necessity of dreams (visions) and goals. If you **have a vision** of what you have been placed on this Earth to accomplish in this lifetime, you have been blessed with a powerful gift. Don't take this God-given gift for granted. It has been given to you, nobody else. It is your responsibility and opportunity to **fulfill your potential.** And until you do, you won't be completely satisfied.

As I have stated earlier, God has designed you for success, and you are destined for greatness, if you learn how to **listen to your inner voice,** which is the vehicle in which you can **communicate to the Ultimate Power – God.** Most people refuse to **listen to this inner guidance system**, choosing to kill the pain, frustration and depression with drugs. All of these mental ailments are nothing more than tools that God is using to wake you up and help steer you onto the correct course for success and happiness.

I have suffered my own "Divine Discontent" more times than I would like to admit. Our lowest time that I can remember happened in Milwaukee. I was working as a starving musician, living one of my childhood dreams, trying to find myself. Ann was traveling with me. I will never forget the day that we sat in a restaurant with one dollar to our names. We were both hungry and had no choice but to order the all-you-can-eat soup special of the day – split pea (I will never forget and have never eaten it since).

Walking out of that restaurant, I was depressed, broke and humiliated, much like some of you might feel right now. At that time I knew I had to **do something.** The pain had become too intense. I immediately took action by quitting the band

and going back to school. If this embarrassing event had not occurred, I might still be a starving musician. But I believe because God had other plans for my life, He knocked me off this false path to find my truer course. He will do that for you if you **have the courage to listen** and **follow your heart.**

We lived through this adventure and many other trials and tribulations, just like you will. In every experience you face, there is a lesson that will help you **advance to the next step on your journey of enlightenment.** In every adversity there is a seed of equal or greater opportunity if you **choose to see it in the positive light of God.**

Every one of us has the choice to react in a negative manner, or **respond with a positive response** to every situation in which we are involved. How we think and act determines how well we will do achieving our dreams. The next story explains it best.

The president of a national shoe manufacturing company had a dream of expanding the market into the Third World countries and decided to send two of his young salesmen to Africa. Their job was to establish new accounts for the company and report back in three months. At the end of the allotted time, the first young man walked into the corporate office and barraged his boss with excuses as to why he had been unsuccessful. He attempted to explain to the wiser gentleman that trying to sell shoes to barefoot natives was not a good idea, and the hardest job he had ever attempted. The beaten-down man continued trying to convince the president that selling shoes to people who didn't wear shoes was impossible. He was dismissed a rejected man.

The boss reluctantly asked to see the second man, expecting to see and hear the same excuses. But, he was pleasantly surprised when the man walked into his office with a sense of pride and enthusiasm he had not seen for many years. The confident young salesman was the opposite of his depressed counterpart, yet they had been assigned to the same area and had been given the same task. His superior asked him why he was so happy. He astounded his boss by informing him "that was the easiest job I have ever had – nobody was wearing shoes – yet!"

Two equally qualified men, same situation and two completely different results – one success and one failure. What was the difference?

Positive Power was the difference. People who **possess the power of positive thinking** and back it up with action

produce remarkable results. Negative thinkers are only going to find an excuse for their failures. Don't **look at your dreams** like the first salesman looked at his.

Re-mind yourself how great your vision was and can be again. You are never too old to **dream great dreams**. Colonel Sanders went on the road to sell his chicken recipe after he received his first Social Security check. It's never too late. Ray Kroc started McDonald's when he was fifty-five years young. Look at your dreams and hopes in a positive light. Imagine how fabulous it will be when you **design your life. Re-member** (put back together) **what gave you passion** – a God-given vision gives you a reason to live!

Don't give me an excuse why you can't dream. **Give me a result.** Give yourself a result. **Get in the habit** of responding to your dreams and daily situations in a positive way. **Use every challenge** as an opportunity to **live the life you want** and not allow negativity to rule your world. Then, and only then will you **be blessed with the power that can make your visions turn into reality.**

"Is anything too hard for the Lord?"

Genesis 18:14

<u>Vision Quest</u>

"I came that they may have life, and may have it abundantly"

Jesus

How many times in your life have you had the chance to **do great things**, including achieving your dream, but were too busy, scared or lazy to pursue the possibility? Many are petrified by the fear of failure, afraid they are one check away from the poorhouse. Instead, you could be one thought away from riches! It is all in how you perceive the situation. What you **focus** on is what you will be. That is a law of nature that no one can change. Do you **concentrate** on survival or success?

I remember the realization of one of my dreams, which was presenting a motivational seminar for Ivy Tech State College. I had this dream for two years before I acted. I finally talked with the lady at the college who gave me the name of the woman I needed to speak to – but for some reason, I didn't. Why? Why do you not **take action toward your dreams?** The reason I didn't make my dream a reality at that time is I let negative thoughts enter my mind and I procrastinated. Has that ever happened to you?

Procrastination is a negative energy. Nobody gets anywhere putting things off. If you are guilty of procrastination, (and who isn't?) it is because you do not believe you can **accomplish the task** and visualize yourself failing. God did not create you to fail. The image of failure is a negative program that has been placed in our heads, not by God, but rather past negative programming. So, instead of at least attempting the project, you don't even try – which is ultimate failure for you, and victory for the dark side. This negative thought stops you cold in your tracks.

Sometimes we don't even know why we procrastinate. It took me another year before I took action on that particular goal. When I look back now and see that it was so simple, I ask myself why I waited for so long.

"Do It Now" has been such an over-used phrase that most people don't understand that these three powerful words are probably the best advice for a person to achieve rebirth. Remember, what you sow, you shall reap. The only way you are going to come alive is to **live again with passion,** and not put off what needs to be done today. By doing something toward your dream every minute possi[ble] you will **feel better about yourself** and your life. You will also **accomplish what you set out to do** if you **refuse to quite until you conquer the challenge.**

It feels great to know that the Positive Power of God is always working. All you have to do is **work with God's power.** You've heard the motto, **"let go, let God".** I am not promising your travels will be smooth. Sometimes things will not go the way you wanted or expected. Most people would call this "wrong", but I personally don't believe in the concept of "right" and "wrong". Everything is for a purpose if you believe that every experience is a lesson to **further your journey on the path of personal truth.**

The Positive Power of God will always win out over negativity if you **choose to use this miraculous power.** The truth is, it's not what happens to us that makes our course. It is how we choose to use or misuse the experience. If you **don't expect** and **only experience** you will **live a heavenly life.** If you judge each event with certain expectations instead of enjoying the experience for what it's worth, you are setting yourself up for disappointment and failure.

...ason many of you have lost your vision is ...appened in your past that was the breaking ...creamed "I quit! I give up!". Maybe it was a business failure, divorce, death of a loved one, losing a job, bankruptcy, society or family pressure. All of us, sometime in our lives, **face this ultimate challenge.** It is different for each of us, but no less devastating for all of us. This God-inspired challenge is going to push you to your limit and beyond. This is the time you must **make the decision to dig in and fight** or give in and give up. You have the choice to **use this situation as an opportunity to grow and be a stronger person** or allow it to destroy you.

One of our ultimate challenges confronted us in 1995. Ann and I had worked hard for twenty years of our lives, building what we thought was a secure business. We owned a nationally-accredited hairdressing school, and two other businesses. We traveled coast-to-coast, working for the major haircare companies. We were treated like royalty, staying at the most luxurious hotels, eating at the finest restaurants and being chauffeured in limousines. We were living on top of the world and then our world came crashing down. Because of bad management, over-expansion, I.R.S.

problems and employee turnover, our empire collapsed. We quickly went from living the great life to the brink of bankruptcy. I tell people now that it was like jumping off of a cliff and not knowing whether we were going to land or crash.

Instead of giving up and taking the negative road, we perceived this situation as a sign that we were not doing what we were destined to do. We saw this catastrophe as an opportunity to start over and rebuild our lives. I knew God had great plans for us. I absolutely knew that I had something inside of me that had to be shared with the world. We had built the previous businesses without too much consideration of His wishes. During this five-year reorganization, Ann and I became partners with God. We put our trust and faith that He was the architect of our lives. He was in the driver's seat. Because of this ultimate trust, He showed me my true path – the one He had planned for me.

Sure, I could have quit. That would have been easy. I could have blamed God and probably did more than once. I could have made accusations and excuses, but why waste my valuable time in such negative activity? I tell you this story, not for you to feel sorry for us, but rather so you can **see that we know where you are or have been**. However low you have been, we've been there. Ann and I have experienced the highest of highs and the lowest lows. We had all of these experiences so we could understand the hurt and frustration you are feeling. We do know where you are coming from and can help you, if you let us.

Whatever has happened, you allowed your dream to be stolen. Nobody can steal your dream until you decide to give up on it. Even after losing everything we had built, we wouldn't let our dream of helping people die. This is what kept us going and still keeps us going today. **Don't ever give up on your dream. Get up** and **take back your dream.** You can **achieve it.** And the amazing secret of resurrecting your life is not whether you **accomplish your dream** because if that was required, then some of you would **succeed** and many would fail. But the truth is, resurrection does not come from the prize for the attainment of the dream. It is "the pursuit of your dream" that will keep you excited and living with passion as you meet each day with enthusiasm. You **have a reason for living** and that gives you new life.

To **reconstruct your dream** is a simple exercise. Every person can accomplish these steps and see their dreams become a reality. But the truth is, less than 10% of the population of the United States will invest the time and effort to use this sure-fire path to happiness. I hope that you are one of the chosen souls that can **see the importance of these words** and **believe in yourself** enough to want to be reborn and will **do something about it.** Talk is cheap. Everybody *wants* to be more successful. Successful people will do what unsuccessful people won't do. Successful people **set goals.** Are you going to **follow this success program?** If you **take the time to do these exercises** it will be the best time you can **invest into your future.**

The feeling you will experience when you accomplish one of your dreams is so powerful. It will give you the confidence that many people don't ever experience. It is an opportunity for you to **pat yourself on the back** and we all need that once in awhile. If you are new to the idea of goal-setting, don't worry. At this point some of you might be questioning whether you can achieve your dreams. **Believe me** – you can.

The secret of this technique is **start as small as you feel comfortable.** You **begin living your God-given dreams** by first conducting a dream session. This is a time that anything goes. The only rule is to **write down everything that comes to your mind that you want to experience, have, be, or give.** Do not judge whether you can or can't, or if it is important or not. That decision will come later. In this part of the exercise you get to dream without limitation. Then, once you have a list of your dreams written down, you will start choosing which is the most important to accomplish at this moment. Once the particular dream is chosen, you will **start setting goals** that are so small that you can **achieve them in one day** and no longer than one week. This way, you **start immediately** receiving positive reinforcement that builds up your confidence in goal-setting and your abilities. Baby steps do work.

You can **do anything you desire** no matter where you are starting. You don't have to have money, a college degree, be a certain color or age to **restore your dreams and hopes,** and really **live life like it was designed to live.** This is the present, and the reason we call it the "present" is because it's God's gift to each of us. What you do with it is always your choice.

You have the opportunity to **live your dreams**; **get out of the rut** and **live with enthusiasm**. It won't be easy. But take a moment and **imagine achieving your first goal.** That first, small victory gives you that support to continue with the next, and the next, and the next, until you **find yourself** standing on top of the mountain, instead of questioning yourself whether you can climb it.

At this time, prepare yourself to write down your dreams. Find a quiet place where you will not be disturbed. You'll need paper and pencils. Instrumental music is helpful to block out surrounding sounds. Before you start, get yourself comfortable; close your eyes, take three deep breaths; **clear your mind** from the trappings of the day; **pray to God** for guidance; be silent and listen and **write down your dreams.** Write the first thing that comes into your mind and **don't prejudge** your thoughts. Fantasize about what you would be doing; what the perfect job or career would be; who you would be; what would the perfect day be; what would you have; where would you live; and who would you love, what would you like to do for God? Don't hold anything back. **Dream BIG!** (Use an extra sheet if needed.) **Try writing for five minutes** without stopping.

"Commit everything you do to the Lord Trust him to help you do it and he will."

Psalms 37:5

MY DREAM SHEET

1. _____
2. _____
3. _____
4. _____
5. _____
6. _____
7. _____
8. _____
9. _____
10. _____
11. _____
12. _____
13. _____
14. _____
15. _____
16. _____
17. _____
18. _____
19. _____
20. _____

Congratulations on achieving your first step to success.

Ask And You Shall Receive...If...

"The Father will give you whatever you ask him in my name"

John 15:16

To **achieve your dreams**, you must **transform them into goals** that are written down in a step-by-step method. If you don't finalize your dreams on paper, then they continue to be only dreams, and all you are is a dreamer. A dreamer is not a "doer". A dreamer is one who fantasizes about what they are going to do someday. The problem is that someday never arrives, and they never find true success and happiness.

Begin your goal-setting process by finding a quiet place that you will not be disturbed. You will need paper, pencils and your list of dreams. Instrumental music is helpful to block out surrounding sounds. Before you start, get yourself comfortable; close your eyes; take three deep breaths; clear your mind from the trappings of the day; pray for guidance; be silent and listen. Next, you should look at your dream sheet and **divide your dreams into different types of goals.**

Look at your sheet and decide which are truly important to you. Be careful not to judge whether they are possible or not. Ask yourself; if you could **achieve just one** of them, which one would it be? Which accomplished dream would create the most impact on your life? Then, decide which one of the following categories your selected dream falls within: Immediate – something that can be achieved this week; Short-term – a dream that can be realized in less than three months; Intermediate – a goal that should be accomplished in the next year; and finally Long-term – a larger dream which would take between three to five years.

Whatever category of time your dream falls within, the only way to make it a reality is through the 5 Steps To Great Goal-Setting. The first of these steps is deciding exactly WHAT you want. While dreaming you didn't have to be specific, but as you set your goals you must **be as specific as you possibly can**, and the more precise the description the better. The size, shape, color, brand and any other way you can **describe your goal** should be written down in a manner that a stranger could visualize it as well as you. The more vividly you can **see it in your mind**, the better your subconscious knows what you want. Remember; what the mind of man can **conceive and believe,** it can **achieve**.

The second step is HOW you will go about accomplishing this task. Goals will not work if you don't **work the goals**. **Use a step-by-step plan** to **attain them**. Goals do not work by magic. I have people tell me how goals didn't work for them. After I question them, I find out why – they didn't **work the goals**. You must **have a blueprint**, just like building a house. You wouldn't dare start building a house and not have plans. Yet we live our lives without direction. No matter how large or small your dream is, make an itinerary of what actions must be achieved to realize the dream.

WHEN is important so your subconscious knows when you are wanting this goal to be transformed into a reality. This step is tricky for some people, because if they do not achieve the goal by that particular time, they think they have failed, and quit trying. Don't do this. Be realistic. The larger the goal, the longer achieving the goal may take. Many times, you might not hit your target on your exact schedule, but **keep going,** even if it takes more time than you planned. You will get better with practice, and I promise you that you will **start hitting your goals** closer to your target time. Always **remember that God has His own timetable. Be patient** and **do whatever you can do today to get one step closer toward your desired outcome**. The reasons for setting time estimates are to be able to check your progress and eliminate procrastination. So don't let the time tables control you. Use them to your best interest. They are there to help you achieve your goals, not get you frustrated.

The FOURTH step of great goal-setting is WHO. This important part of the formula is not mentioned in many goal-setting programs, and I believe is one of the more important. Finding out who can help you **achieve your particular goal** will make it go smoother. The obvious answer is asking for God's help and the guidance of The Holy Spirit. You can do this by starting every morning with "Good Morning, God!" instead of "Good God, it's morning!"

I still remember the first teacher that crossed my path. His name was Dr. Hand, and he sure did give us a hand. He was my inspiration and was the first who introduced me to my destiny, although at that time I didn't understand. I will never forget his daily greeting, "top of the morning!" He was a Godly man. He was sent to guide me and teach me the way. I thank him for that. There are people who will cross your path who can teach you the way and **cut down your time and effort**...if you **ask.** Trial and error are okay, but they are expensive and slow. Why try to reinvent the wheel when there are people available who have already done it? There are many successful people who are willing to help you. All you have to do is **ask in a positive, enthusiastic manner**, and many of them will be honored you asked them. Use O.P.E. (other people's experience) and you are on the shortcut to hitting your goal.

WHY is the last, but no less important, ingredient. The answer of why you are wanting to accomplish this particular goal is what will keep you going when you are ready to throw in the towel. Your "Why" gives you the real reason you are putting up with the pain and frustration. It is the strongest motivator you possess. **Never forget why you are wanting to achieve your goal** – to fulfill God's purpose through you, and that is a strong enough Why that you will **never stop working on accomplishing it**. And that is the secret to everlasting achievement – keeping that fire burning as you **climb the mountain of life** to **conquer your quest.**

"I have set before you life and death, blessing and cursing; therefore choose life, that thou and they seed may live."

Deuteronomy 30:19

<u>Seek and Ye Shall Find</u>

"Behold, I stand at the door and knock; if anyone hears my voice, and opens the door, I will enter..."

Revelation 3:20

The quickest way for you to **feel the rush of excitement** run through your veins is to have a particular goal that has you jumping out of bed every morning to try to accomplish. The lack of this goal is the reason so many people are not living. They are still breathing, walking, and talking, but they have no passion. Let the dead bury the dead. **Don't worry** about what others are doing or saying. **Start on this program immediately, recreate your life** and **change your world.**

To accomplish this, you must **write down your goals.** Do you have your goals written down yet? If you are like most people, you haven't taken the time, or don't believe it will make a difference. But wait – **don't go on until you have written your goals down.** If you proceed without this important step, you are just reading another book, wasting your valuable time, dreaming that this book is going to bring you back to life. That will not happen.

Nobody can resurrect you but you. **Breathe new life into your body. Seek the Kingdom of Heaven.** It is at hand. All you have to do is **seek it** and you will **find it**. The lack of this seeking is the reason you died in the first place. You must **listen to your heart**. You can no longer live by someone else's dreams. The only way that you can **experience life** is to do it to the sound of your own drum.

To **rescue yourself** out of the life you have been living you must **take a chance. Go for the gusto. Go for broke.** You must now **take a risk** and **seek out what is really important to you**. What's it going to hurt to **express your ideas** using the Five Steps To Great Goal-Setting and writing them down? You have probably heard before how important this exercise is; but do you know why it is important?

I have personally proven that if I can get myself to write down a goal and follow the steps I have revealed, with God's help, the goal will be achieved. I'm not stating that just because you **write something down** on paper that the goal automatically happens – we wish. But, I do believe that if you **ask** and **seek** by taking action, you will **receive**. There is something magical about writing down your goals as specific as possible.

This magical happening has to do with your subconscious mind. This deeper area of your brain, called your silent partner, is an amazing tool, and if used properly, can help you **achieve whatever you desire** and sincerely believe you can attain it. The action of writing a specific goal triggers a no-fail plan to your subconscious mind, which will work on your request 24 hours a day, without you having to consciously think about it. That is why it is called the 'silent partner.'

You might be questioning this secret power that God has given to each and every one of us. Let me ask you some questions that I think will help you realize the power of this sleeping giant. Have you ever seen someone that you have known for years but you can't remember their name? I know every person has had this experience. What is the first question you silently ask yourself? Is it not something like; "what is their name?" Why do we ask our self this question? You have already tried remembering the name and couldn't. Yet, for some reason you still ask this question to yourself. Why?

When you ask yourself this question, you are asking your subconscious to help you. Your mind is a library that has recorded every piece of knowledge, event, and relationship you have ever experienced. By asking your silent partner what the name is, you have started a searching process that will not stop until it has matched a name with a face and given you the answer. And, as you know and have probably experienced, it might take days before you get the answer. But, it always happens. When you are not thinking about it, the name you asked for pops into your mind. How did it appear out of nowhere to now here? Why do you know it now, and didn't know it when you needed it?

Your subconscious mind is a tireless worker and will **stay on a project until it is completed**. If you tell it precisely what you desire, give it directions for how to do it, and believe it will help you accomplish it, this marvelous machine will start working with you on your chosen task. It will steer you in the right direction, show you things you might have missed and keep working diligently until you have achieved your goal – if you wrote one down.

I know that some of you are thinking that you don't have to write your goals down for this to work. You might argue that you can simply think about it.

A study on goal-setting was conducted by Harvard University that tracked a graduating class for twenty years. Before leaving school, every graduate was asked if they had their goals written down in an orderly fashion. Only 3% of the graduates were able to present their written goals. There were another 10% who had goals in their minds, but they weren't written down. The largest group of 60% knew what they wanted to do but didn't have any goals. The other 25% didn't know. The results after twenty years were that the 3% who had written goals were more financially successful than the other 97% combined! You be the judge.

This might sound 'too good to be true' but it is a fact. I know this incredible power is there for the asking, and I use it every day. The subconscious is like a muscle. It needs to be exercised. When you first **start using this power** the results might not be as fast as you want, but don't lose faith. **Believe in the power of the subconscious mind**. Realize that it is one of the most powerful tools that God has given you to **achieve your dreams. Keep working it daily** and like any other muscle it will **get stronger.**

A good example that compares the mind to a muscle is in a personal story. Because I had been doing so much teaching and writing, my muscles were losing their strength, which is called atrophy. It is caused by lack of use. I had been using my mind muscle so much that I had not taken time to keep my other muscles in prime shape. Because I **believe in balance**, I knew this was an area of concern that needed immediate attention. I decided I would start with push-ups as part of my regimen. The first night I struggled to do six, and collapsed on the floor, unable to do one more. I skipped one night to let my muscle repair itself and I tried again. This time I did eight push-ups. I continued this exercise ritual and was pleasantly surprised that every time I did this exercise, my muscle was stronger. I was always able to do a few more push-ups.

With use, every part of our body, including our mind, gets stronger. Work it, then rest it, then work it, and it will keep getting stronger for you. If you don't use it, you will lose it; and the mind is a terrible thing to waste. By setting goals, you are exercising your mind. You are stretching its limits. You are challenging its power. That is exactly what you and your mind need in order to **resurrect your life**.

Whether you believe it or not, your subconscious is doing its job every minute of the day. If you don't **control your mind**, then outside forces will do it for you. You have the choice, and every choice you make determines your destiny. **Think** about it. Are you controlling your mind, or is it controlling you?

Get control of your mind. Take control of your life. Put your mind to work on what you want out of life. **Invest the time to write down your goals.** If it doesn't better your life, then you will be right where you are now. But imagine if a small thing like writing down your goals truly worked, and opened the door that you have been searching for? Where could you possibly be? What could you possibly be doing? What are you doing now is not satisfying you, or you wouldn't be reading this book. You are looking for more. You have so much to gain. **Go for it.** You can't lose.

It is astounding that such a simple exercise can produce such amazing results, but I have seen it and experienced the magic of goal-setting. Put your goals down in black and white. **Commit them to the world**. For every action there is a reaction. When you **take the risk** of ridicule by letting out your dreams and expressing your desire, you have set into motion a universal energy that will help you **recreate your life**; and that is what you want, isn't it?

Get to work. Don't delay. If you didn't do it yesterday, don't worry. That time is past and you can't relive your past. Your past doesn't equal your future. It's not what you have done. It's what you are going to do. **Don't wait** until tomorrow because it is never here. You can **live the life that you dream**. No matter what has happened to you in your past, this is the first day of the rest of your life. Start it out right by getting in the habit of practicing the art of goal-setting. **Believe in goal-setting** and **do it now!**

"If you can **believe**, all things are possible to him who believes.

Mark 9:23

5 STEPS TO GREAT GOAL-SETTING

WHAT:
_____
_____
_____

WHEN:
_____
_____
_____

HOW:
_____
_____
_____

WHO:
_____
_____
_____

WHY:
_____
_____
_____

Remember: Goals are as essential to success as air is to life.

It All Comes Down To Attitude

"All things can be done for the one who believes"

Mark 9:23

I will ask you the question one more time; have you written down your goals yet? I know, I'm really testing your patience, but talk is cheap. It takes action to **bring yourself back to life.** Now is the time to **prove to yourself,** your family, and to the world that you **believe in yourself,** in God and in the working of Positive Power. If you have a positive attitude and **believe in these words**, you understand how important this step really is. If you can't be motivated to take this simple step, how do you expect to **follow through** on anything else?

If you now **possess the Positive Power of God** you will see the possibility of this technique working for you and you'll not have a problem completing this goal-setting exercise. But, if there is negative programming in your mind, you will have doubt and hesitation, which causes lack of action. Which of these attitudes are you feeling? Listen to your inner voice. Are you hesitating about writing your goals down? Do you know that you should but for some reason you can't?

You are either the master or the victim of your attitude. You always have a choice regarding your attitude. If you **vote yes to a positive attitude**, you are on the road to greatness. Your life will be full of possibilities or limitations; it all comes down to your attitude.

What does attitude mean, anyway? Attitude is a state or condition of mind. It is the way you think about life – about God. It is a habitual mode of regarding everything you experience. It is your approach to and perspective on life. Your emotions, temperament, and disposition are controlled by your attitude – or the way you view every situation in which you're involved. It reflects what you are thinking. Your attitude is the beginning of creation or destruction. It is always your choice.

God gave man the power of choice. Choosing a positive attitude requires courage because you are choosing to **respond constructively to every challenge** that life presents to you. A positive attitude is the prescription for success.

After this explanation of attitude, you can see why a positive attitude makes a major difference. Your view of life determines how alive you are going to feel. If your attitude is negative, it will make your picture of life the worst and prevent you from living your life with the passion of positive expectancy. By assuming a positive stance, you believe that you can **accomplish your dreams**, which is essential to resurrecting your life. Life can be a blessing or a curse, heaven or hell, and it all comes down to the attitude that you carry in your mind.

Once you **understand the Positive Power of God** and **know that He is with you at all times,** you are more confident. With improved self-confidence you will **picture the possibility** of living your dreams and move toward them with anticipation. When you are certain about the outcome because of your faith in God and yourself, doubt does not cloud your mind. Instead, the positive vibration gives a clear vision of your choice, the reward, and the certainty you are achieving your goals.

Some of you are not going to agree with this next statement, but it is true. You <u>are</u> where you are at this time, and doing what you are doing, because of the thoughts that **control your mind.**

Sixty-thousand thoughts go through an average person's mind every day, yet only one thought controls your mind at one time. That thought is either positive or negative, which is putting you in either a negative, disempowered state, OR in a positive, empowered state of mind. These thoughts are what make up your attitude. If you don't invest the energy and time to **keep the negative weeds out of the garden of your mind**, these disempowering thoughts will paralyze you, and you will be a member of "the walking dead".

Think of your mind as a car engine. When it is running smoothly, firing on all cylinders, the car moves smoothly toward its destination. But, as soon as one misfire (negative) enters the engine, it affects the performance and capability of the engine. The mind is no different. Every positive thought improves your mental power. A negative spark makes you hesitate. Too many negative thoughts programmed together will stop you.

One way or the other you are making a choice. If you procrastinate making the decision to be positive, you have chosen to be negative. If you do nothing about improving your relationship with love, discovering your inner power and choosing positive thoughts, then you have selected the negativeway of life.

It takes no energy to be negative. A large part of the human race is negative. A person can easily live in this state of darkness, but by taking the trampled, well-worn path, the unfortunate soul will never experience its truth. This is what happens when a person quits on life. You will never live the life you could have realized, persisting in this gloomy state of depression.

A positive, self-confident, Christ-conscious attitude is the best asset you can possess. The Positive Power of God will help you resurrect yourself faster than anything else. When you **look at the world in a loving manner**, the whole world changes for the better. It will help you **develop your life in a constructive manner**.

Negative thoughts can never be building blocks of starting a new life. All of us have experienced negative influences on our lives. Have they gotten you where you want to be?

Every human being has the ability and God-given right to develop whatever attitude they choose. Don't try telling me you were born with a certain attitude. Our attitudes are not passed through the genes, so don't blame your parents. Attitude is nothing more than a mere habit of thought, and habits can be acquired, developed and changed.

The first step in changing your attitude is awareness. **Examine your attitude** by listening to yourself when you are talking to others, evaluating whether you are reacting (negative) or responding (positive) to your daily situations. **Listen to the words you use**. If you are serious about changing your attitude and habits, **keep a journal** for a few days to **record the words you use.**

The following list of words signal that you might have a negative attitude that needs some adjustment:

BUT – This negative word is used in sentences to explain the excuse you have made as to why you can't do something, for example: I would love to go, *but,* I have to watch the kids". Instead of using the word "but", substitute the word "and". This positive word, when substituted, is a better action word. "I would love to go AND I'm watching the kids, so they can go with us". What a noticeable change, and only one word was replaced. Just think how many things you could accomplish if you replaced all your 'buts' with 'ands.'

Remember to **get off your** '**buts and butts**', **get on your feet**, and **put your rear** in **gear**. That's how to **take back your life** and **make it what you want it to be**. The only way that this is going to happen is with the Positive Power of God!

If you are one of 'the walking dead' (and you should know after you have monitored yourself, as previously suggested), the next step is to **admit** you are negative. There is nothing you can do about your attitude even one second ago, but you are responsible for every thought that goes through your mind from here on out, because you now **know you have a choice**.

So many people understand and even agree that Positive Power would be better for them, but they tell themselves and others they CAN'T. Can't means either you don't want to, or you don't know how. If you don't know how, you can learn. Change the statement, "I can't swim" to "I don't know how to swim, and I would love to learn". If CAN'T means you don't want to do something, then express it in those terms. There is not a problem with not wanting to do something. If you decide not to do it, just explain "I really don't want to do that".

With this change of wording and a new attitude, you are no longer a victim. You are in **control of your life.** You are in charge and you have choices. You can do it! I know it. Do you **believe you can change**?

If you say you can't be positive, is it because you don't want to, or you don't know how? If you don't know how, then keep reading because this material will teach you how. If you don't want to **learn to live with Positive Power** and **resurrect your life** into something beautiful and meaningful, then you are reading the wrong book and wasting your time.

"Yeah, but what <u>IF</u>?" This question has probably popped into your mind. It is that negative chatterbox inside your head trying to get you to give up. It doesn't want to lose its royal position of control over you, and it knows that if you learn to be positive, it is going to be shoved back into the darkness. I've heard all the excuses - "If I had been taller, bigger, richer, younger, luckier, a different color, etc., I would have done it." How many times do you hear the excuses of why someone did not live their dreams? I see many people who 'could have been, should have been, would have been, but weren't.' So many people use the word "if" as an excuse; as *if* that gets them off the hook and relieves them from the torment of knowing they are not truly living. My best reply to them is; don't give me an excuse – **give me a result**.

To **perform the miracle of resurrection**, you must **produce results**. The only way to **produce a result** is to **believe in God** and in yourself and **use Positive Power** to **take action. Get the I-CAN attitude**. That stands for Improvement – Constant And Never-Ending. By using this method of thinking you are always learning, striving to be your best, and knowing that every day you are getting better and better, and getting closer to your goal. And it doesn't matter how much you **improve each day**. It is only important that you do **improve every day,** and you can do it. Inch-by-inch, anything is a cinch.

When you are green, you grow and when you are ripe, you rot. Make sure you are learning and experiencing new things every day. This way, you are green and not rotting. **Stretch yourself out of your comfort zone. Try something exciting**. Whatever you do, **learn something new** and you will soon be alive and kicking, with a sense of awareness and vitality much like what you had as a child. Wouldn't you like that? Who wouldn't?

Are you ready, willing and able to **bring yourself back to life** – to **live the life you have always dreamed**? Are you ready to **make your dream come true**? Are you really ready? Many people think they are ready, but they never **get going.** Just getting ready will not get you what you want. Too many people are walking around, ready and waiting. They are waiting to hit the lottery or retire. They falsely believe and desperately hope that their ship will arrive, but they never sent their ship out. You must not only be ready, but you must **be willing.**

You must be willing to **sacrifice**. You must **be prepared** to start building today for a better tomorrow. Whether it is time, money or effort, you must invest it today for your future dreams. But the good news is, when you **invest in yourself**, it always pays the highest interest. **Believe in yourself** enough to **invest whatever it takes** to **live your dreams.**

Many students ask me what kind of sacrifice it will take. I always give them the same answer; "if you are really serious about living your dreams, you will **do whatever it takes**, as long as you **do no harm** to another of God' creations. I also tell them that successful people do what unsuccessful people *won't* do. If you are truly dedicated to your awakening from the "walking dead", you will **do whatever it takes**, for as long as it takes.

You must also **be willing to take the heat**. Whenever you move, there is friction. The faster you move the more friction is created. And friction produces heat. You must produce friction, and thus heat, to make a move. I am referring to the kind of heat you are going to receive when you are ridiculed because you are trying something new. Heat comes when people talk about you and cause problems because you are getting ahead, and they are not. You will be the 'lucky one'.

You will lose friends. I know, because it happened to us. But they have the choice, just like you. Just because your friends want to stay where they are, should not mean that you have to sacrifice your life for their friendship. If they are true friends, they will be proud of you for wanting to **do more with your life.** I'm sorry to report that most of the time, the negative thoughts of jealousy and anger rear their ugly head. Be prepared for it and understand there are many others out there who think and believe like you and will love to be your new friends.

You must be able to withstand the negative forces that will try to stop you. These unseen deterrents will be present every step of your journey. You must be able to see through these negative smokescreens and **keep on keeping on toward your dreams**. You must be able to **overlook small thinkers** who will gossip about you. Let them say what they want. When they are talking about you, and you are creating a stir, you know you are on track. **Remember,** small minds talk about people, average minds talk about events, and great minds talk about ideas. The Positive Power of God will help you outlast the negative, and you will **reach your ultimate dream** if you **have faith** and **take action**.

You can do it if you **keep the attitude in a positive state**. You cannot afford the luxury of a negative thought. One negative thought is like a cancer. It keeps growing if you don't nip it in the bud. Eliminate it with the words of Jesus. When you start getting a negative thought just **think about love.** Love is the strongest energy and it will **eliminate that negative thought**.

What the mind of man can conceive and _believe_ he can achieve. If you continue thinking the word 'love', you are focusing on 'love'. You become what you constantly focus on. The more intense this thought, the closer to Christ-consciousness you will become. That is the ultimate goal.

My challenge to you is to **start today learning a new way to think**; a new way to **live with the Positive Power of God**. **Start clearing your mind** of the negative garbage and **concentrate on only positive thoughts** for one day. If you need to start with a shorter period of time, try an hour, or even a minute. **Be aware of each and every thought** entering your mind. **Learn how to control your mind** instead of it controlling you.

Your attitude comes from the thought processes in your mind. At this very moment you are thinking either a positive or negative thought. You do this thought process approximately 60,000 times a day. Since each one of these thoughts affect your attitude and performance, which thought do you prefer?

Of course, the majority of people, if not all, would prefer a positive thought. However, in today's society, this idea of a positive state of mind is being lost. Ask the next ten people you meet how they feel today and record their answers. You will hear a barrage of sicknesses, excuses, and problems. Some might say they're doing 'okay'. But how many people are doing great and **answer with enthusiasm?**

The epidemic of negativity we are experiencing is proof that our mind is manipulating us, and we are not controlling our thoughts. And the only way to have the positive attitude that most of us desire is to **take back control of our minds**. We have been programmed by the sin of negativity for a life of slavery, instead of enjoying the Kingdom that is within us.

When you decide to **use the Positive Power of God** and **live by the words of Jesus Christ**, you will **eliminate the darkness of negativity** from your mind and you will **discover the 'love' attitude** that is unstoppable!

"As we have therefore opportunity, let us **do good unto all men**."

Galatians 6:10

<u>You Can Change</u>

"Take delight in the Lord and he will give you the desires of your heart"

Psalms 37:4

You might be thinking to yourself; "I can't do all this stuff". And if you are thinking this negative thought, I want to tell you that you <u>*can*</u> if you want to; **believe it works** and don't be afraid of trying something new. Remember, this new exercise – **eliminate the negative word** (can't) and **replace it with the power of the positive (love)**. Stop and evaluate the impact of the change - "I *love* to do this stuff". This one change will drastically change your life.

I'll never forget the first time I heard the Rev. Robert Schuller ask the question, "what would you do if you knew you couldn't fail?". I was mesmerized by the catchy, memorable jingle. I immediately understood the power in these words. I started thinking more seriously about the challenge. What <u>*would*</u> I do if I knew I could not fail – *really*? Could I even ask my mind to calculate such a possibility, or was my mind, like so many others, clouded with a fog of negative, limited thoughts that would stop such outlandish dreaming? I didn't think I was negative, yet I hadn't accomplished everything I had dreamed of doing. Why?

The truth is that most of us don't go for the gold, striving to be not just good, but being the very best that we can possibly be. Few of us push ourselves to use every ounce of creativity and energy we possess, challenging our bodies and minds to the ultimate degree. We always hold back, never putting 110% into whatever we are doing, as though we are saving some energy for a back-up purpose.

A monk once taught me an example of how we always stop short, believing we have used up all of our energy. And, as he showed me, the truth is that we always have more untapped potential if we **challenge ourselves to do our best**. He asked me to do as many push-ups as I could do. He counted twenty and I collapsed on the floor, thinking that was all I could do. Then he challenged me by saying he knew I could do more than what I thought. He asked me to try again and he was right – I did five more push-ups (an additional 25% more than I originally thought I good do).

What else do we quit on too early, thinking we can't go another step? How do you **know what you really are capable of achieving**? Do we not place a mental barrier on ourselves? Are you using your full potential or do you have a roadblock to success?

Possibility and impossibility lie in the perception of the mind. Do you **believe your dream is possible?** Has anybody else already proven that it is humanly possible?

Roger Bannister made history by breaking through the negative thinking that one mile could not be ran in under four minutes. Runners, experts, and doctors all agreed that it was humanly impossible to accomplish this athletic feat, going as far as to state that the heart would explode. And everybody confirmed this thought, until Roger Bannister proved all of them wrong when he unknowingly broke this self-imposed barrier, running himself into history as the first man who ran the "impossible" under-four-minute mile. Immediately after this famous runner proved to the world that it was possible, other athletes started accomplishing the challenge. Nothing had changed except people's minds, which had been holding them back from doing great things. They didn't get stronger or smarter. There was a change in thinking – knowing they could do it instead of questioning themselves.

Can you **accomplish your dream?** If someone else has done what you want to do, then you can **do it.** What would you like to do, but think you can't? Thoughts are powerful and they will stop you, if you allow them.

Here is a personal example; when I told an educated, executive client I was getting prepared to participate in my first "fire walk", where I was going to walk barefoot across hot coals, he threw a barrage of reasons why I was an idiot for attempting such a ridiculous feat. "Don't you know that your skin burns at that high temperature? You'll burn your feet and not be able to walk or work. What if you fall and burn your body? Do you know how painful burns are to heal?"

I tried not listening to such negative garbage, but was unable to block his verbal assault. Before I could protect myself, these negative thoughts locked into my mind. I now had a 'mind-virus.' Every time I thought about doing the fire walk, his words would come into my mind. To eliminate these disempowering words, I informed myself how many children, and adult men and women with skin just like me had already accomplished walking across fire. They were no different than I was, and I knew for a fact that I could conquer this challenge – and I did.

But, what if I had not had the personal power to wipe out his negative comments? These words could have influenced me and kept me from experiencing a thrill of my lifetime! He was wrong. I proved he was overreacting. Yet, his negativity could have stopped me, had I let it. Think back in your life and ask yourself if you have let someone's words or actions stop you from living your dream.

To **recreate your life**, you must **stop your 'stinking thinking'**. To **reclaim your God-given right of living the life you desire** instead of existing in a life you can't stand, you must **eliminate your negative thinking** and **stop listening to negative doomsayers**. How many times have parents, teachers, friends, and society told you how you couldn't do what you wanted to do? Most of us have heard these negative comments since childhood. How can these people judge what you can and can't do? How do they know? Who is telling you that you can't **do what you want to accomplish?**

Is it you? Are you stopping yourself from success and happiness? Do you not **believe that you can accomplish your dream**? Are you too scared to try? Don't want to **take a risk?** Believe me, if you honestly answer 'yes' to these questions, you are in a large majority of people. It is your decision because it is your life. But, if you **know inside there is something else for you**, then you are cheating your soul if you don't at least try to **live the path of your true purpose**. Living your true purpose will not only resurrect you, but it will give you an enlightened life that you can't even imagine.

After you read this paragraph, close your eyes and **imagine** the answers to the following questions. What is the perfect life for you? What would it be like? How would you spend your day? What type of work would you do? Who would you spend it with? Where would you be living? What would be the perfect day... the perfect hour....the perfect moment? Sit back now; close your eyes, relax and imagine.

After designing your perfect life, find someone who has done something similar to what you desire. Don't listen to anybody who isn't an accomplished goal-setter and positive thinker. Be careful. A negative person who might truly think they are "helping" will throw water on your blazing fire. Use a positive person as a mentor or guide to help you **learn the secrets** of how they accomplished the feat that you would like to achieve. This person might not be easy to find so **start now making all the contacts you can**. Networking is very important in meeting the right person. By you possessing Positive Power, they will not be able to resist your energy. Find a way that you are giving to them and they will have plenty to **give back in return.**

When you **have the power of positive vibrations**, the doors will be easier to open. Successful people love Positive Power. Be like a volcano. A volcano is a mountain that is a shaker and mover. It becomes alive. It turns on. It radiates a glow. It's happening. People give attention to a volcano. People give respect to a volcano because it is too hot to handle. It spreads heat. Nothing can stop it. And woe to any person or thing that tries to stand in its way. If you want people to pay attention to you, you are going to have to be a one-man (or woman) spectacular.

So, for you to **change** and **get the respect** of successful people, you need to **maintain a magnetic INNER-glow.** You do this by having the Positive Power of God within you.

You **love yourself.** You **feel on top of the world** because you **know that you are one of God's miracles.** You **love everybody** you meet. You **see them as God's children** also and **recognize the love in them.**

By having this inner-glow, you **radiate an energetic OUTER-glow. Let your love flow. Smile with your eyes!** You can't hide God's enthusiasm. If you are thinking only positive thoughts, there is no choice but to **produce positive vibrations** which make others feel special. They will desire to be with you. They will quickly **realize that you make them feel better** than the negative people with whom they are usually affiliated. When you display these positive vibrations to the correct people, you have a key which will unlock many doors on your path to success.

Unlocking these doors and finding the people who can help you live the life you have always dreamed, will take work on your part. The secret is to **do more service** than anyone else is willing or able to do for every person. **Think of new ways to help** those who help you want in return. **Do this without thought of the benefits** you will receive for yourself. **Show them you sincerely want to help them,** and they will feel more obligated to help you in return.

Remember, this service can not be regular, expected, routine service. You've got to **give them OUTSTANDING, OVERWHELMING service.**

The most outstanding example of this 'give more' attitude is dear to my heart. It is a story about my wife - Ann, of whom I am very proud. After our children were grown, Ann experienced a time in her life that was difficult for many housewives. She hadn't worked outside the home for twenty years. Because she had no current resume, very few organizations wanted to hire her – to their later disappointment. After five months of constant pursuit, she was hired as a part-time homemaker for the local hospital. Her job was to go to the homes of elderly people and help them keep house.

It was a thankless job from an outsider's view, but not for Ann. She was determined to prove everybody had been wrong about her. She went into every home and did far more than was required. She was cursed at, yelled at, called a liar (which she hates the most), and refused health benefits for the entire first year, even though she had been working a scheduled 35-40 hours every week. But nothing stopped Ann from doing the absolute best job she could possibly do.

Because of her valiant effort, these elderly people started slowly realizing that Ann was for real. She was there every week with a positive attitude and a heart of gold. They began sharing their stories with their new friend; someone who would listen with love. Today, Ann is respected in not only the hospital where she works, but she is becoming a legend, as confirmed when a visiting nurse from another hospital crossed paths with her at a patient's home. When Ann introduced herself to the professional, the lady smiled knowingly; "Oh, so you are the Ann Weber we hear so much about. Your patients just love you".

Ann has learned so much from these sages of humanity. I have been blessed that I too enjoy their wisdom and spiritual growth through the stories I am told.

Today, a year later, Ann feels guilty about getting paid for what she does. It is no longer a job; it's a calling. And it began with a job that nobody else wanted (and over 25 people had quit just that year). What Ann added to the situation is the Positive Power of God. She is inspired and protected by the Holy Spirit. She selflessly gave everything, not expecting a thing in return. This is where all of us must begin.

To do this extraordinary service, to resurrect yourself and **change your life to the life you have always dreamed**, is going to take unlimited energy. This is a characteristic found in all tremendously successful people. To achieve this powerhouse of energy, follow the advice of William James, one of America's leading psychologists, who said that feeling follows acting – so to **FEEL energetic, ACT energetic! Do the things you ought to do**, even when (especially when) you don't feel like it – and you'll find you have plenty of energy to do them. **Do it NOW!** You can **change**!

You might be thinking "how am I going to to do that? I'm too tired". You are tired because you are bored. Fatigue is caused by boredom, anxiety, worry, sense of guilt, and other negative patterns hidden in your subconscious. With the Positive Power of God you can **wash those negative thoughts out** and **reinforce your mind with positive habits**. Then you will **see an abundance of energy return into your body**. And until it comes back I tell people to fake it until you make it. **Act like you have energy** and it won't be long before you won't have to fake it any longer.

To **rescue your life** and **return to the awakened world** you must **have the willpower to change**. You can have anything you want if you are willing to pay the price. You just can't have everything. Willpower is the willingness to **pay the price** – whatever it is – in sacrifice, money, time, effort, or any other way in which the price of success must be paid! It is the relentless driving, irresistible determination to **achieve your dreams and goals**, regardless of what stands in your way.

So, to change, you must **have willpower** and persistence. President Calvin Coolidge said "Nothing will take the place of persistence. Talent will not; nothing is more common than unsuccessful men with talent. Genius will not; unrewarded genius is almost a proverb. Education will not; the world is full of educated derelicts. Persistence and determination alone are omnipotent. The slogan 'press on' has solved, and always will solve, the problems of the human race.".

Persistence, determination and willpower will solve your problems. Don't feel discouraged when you are so low you have to **reach up** to touch bottom. Many people have brought themselves out of living death to a life of abundance. You can do it, too. The biggest stars come out at the darkest hour.

To help you **develop energy and positive attributes** you need to **stay around positive, successful, happy people.** You must **stay strong** as you **continue your journey** or you will fall back into the trap of negative thinking. We pick up other people's habits without knowing it. You can't afford to be around negative people who put garbage into your mind. Your mind is not a garbage dump. You must **understand that the mind is a marvelous machine** and is so receptive, it records everything it experiences. The only way that you can make absolutely sure your mind is recording positive input is to stay around positive people; to **read motivational material,** including the Bible, and **to listen to self-help programs.**

If you are working in a negative environment, listen to CDs in your car while you are driving to work. Whenever you get stressed or negative at work, **take five minutes to meditate**. A great place to do this is in the restroom. I also suggest reading positive material and meditating every morning when you arise, and every evening before bed. This habit places your mind in a positive state to rest better and starts your thinking every day in a positive light before the challenges of the day. A friend of ours, Dr. Hand, used to greet us every morning with "top of the morning!". I think that says it so well – it *is* the top of the morning. It *is* a new beginning. It *is* the beginning of your new life. **Start every morning with God and a positive thought**.

If you are doubting the validity of these ideas, remember how long you sing the last song you heard on the radio. Some people have nightmares after viewing a horror movie. Your mind does focus on the last thought you give it. Because of this fact, another good idea is to complete a 'Things to Do' list prior to bedtime. By doing this daily exercise, your subconscious will help you **arrange your thoughts and schedule for the next day**, and it will be easier for you

Another important change you should make immediately is to **eliminate the negative media** from your life. It's always negative news, such as murder, airplane crashes and hostility that make the front-page headlines. The papers and television are full of negative news. How can you **feel excited and positive** about getting up in the morning if you know you have these problems facing you? How much of it can you change anyway? This negative programming on a daily basis is why you died in the first place. Unconsciously, you bought into this negative living. Don't let yourself be brainwashed. You are destined to **be great** and you can change. You **have the power.** You are going to have to **fight for the right to live** and your life is worth it. Isn't it?

Change starts with you. Do you remember the Michael Jackson song "Man in the Mirror"? If we want to **change the world**, we need to **look in the mirror** and must first **be concerned about changing ourselves**. Too many people worry about what is happening outside of their lives. You can't control or change what is happening around the world, but you do have the power to **change one person's life – yours**. Then you can **help educate and motivate one other person** to believe in themselves and the Positive Power of God. That is the way to **change the world** – one person at a time – and it starts with you. One small stone still makes a ripple in even the biggest body of water.

Every action in this universe causes a reaction. You can **make a difference** if you are coached, directed and motivated to **be your best**. Just **stay focused** and **create the light of Positive Power around you.** You won't believe how much you really can **change the world**. Remember though, the first step starts with you, and it is one gigantic step for mankind.

Once you **breathe in this new thinking** and **resurrect yourself,** you will **become a magnet of positive energy** that possesses a unique power that attracts people who need your help. This positive aura will be felt by people who will want to be around you. But first, you must **eliminate as many negative vibrations as possible**, because they deplete this power of attraction. Think about it; would you rather be involved with a positive, enthusiastic person, or a negative, complaining one? Which type of personality makes you feel better?

All of us have to venture out and face our society, which is mostly negative. We fight an uphill battle to stay positive and enthusiastic as the barrage of negative energy attacks and tries to discourage us every day. I hear people question why it seems like it keeps getting harder to cope. Many weaker souls get tired of this daily onslaught of evil. They submit to these negative thoughts and give up their hope for happiness.

These lost souls don't understand what they have sacrificed. Once they surrender to the negative pressure, they lose their energy and zest for life. These members of the walking dead accept the negative thinking because it is the easiest path. They fail to realize their true path of life will never be easy. This wide path that they have chosen is never as difficult as the narrow journey – where the real truth is always discovered. These sad souls silently realize deep down inside what they have given up, but don't believe they **have the courage** and energy to fight back and regain what was once their God-given life.

Some try to **recapture the feeling of freedom** again but find that it is too difficult to break out of the bondage of their daily negative habits. It would take too much work, too much risk, so they become another member of the 'walking dead'. They have sold their soul in exchange for the easy life. This one decision has doomed them to a life of living death. Their life goes on, but the thrill of living is gone.

The secret to a wonderful life is to **be productive** and to **accomplish something which will better the human race**. When a sense of unimportance takes over a person the soul withers, but the God-spark never diminishes completely. Its whisper still deeply resonates though the message of pain, bitterness and sorrow. There is always hope!

If you find yourself in this situation, the great news is – you can **live again**! You can shout "give me liberty or give me death" much like our forefathers shouted when they were fighting for their independence. **Make this your Independence Day**. As Jesus said, "I am the resurrection and the Life" I am saying to you "<u>you</u> are the resurrection and the Life" for your life. To **change your life**, you must **change**. God will help.

How do you change? **Change your thoughts** and you can **change anything.** The world in which you live now is not determined by outward circumstance nearly as much as by your inner thoughts, which habitually occupy your mind. One of the wisest men who ever lived – Marcus Aurelius, said "A man's life is what his thoughts make of it.". The Bible scripture says "as a man thinketh in his heart, so is he" - Proverbs 23:7.

First, you must truly **decide you want to live again.** Once you **make that decision**, you **confront every negative situation with a positive thought**, knowing that as long as you don't give up, you will **live life to the fullest. Understand that this choice will be hard**, but struggle brings strength. Every experience is the process of learning the lessons of life. Know that you will be in the minority, because most people are only existing, sleepwalking through life, missing the beauty of every waking moment.

These people who have lost their purpose come from every walk of life. There is no part of society where there aren't victims suffering from this tragic dis-ease. Even reborn Christians who have claimed Jesus as their Savior, are not immune to this affliction. You don't have to put up with it. You can **recreate your life** and **lift yourself out of the rut of negativity.** It takes time, effort, persistence, determination, belief, and a positive attitude, but it can be done, no matter what your race, sex, age or income. Yet many people will never **feel this wonderful feeling of living again** because they refuse to be open-minded enough to try living the life that I cherish.

If you truly want to change, you should at least **try these ideas for thirty days.** Allow the roots to have time to take hold. **Make sure the ideas get planted in good soil** (positive thoughts). The parable that Jesus taught in Matthew 13 explains it best:

"**Listen!** A farmer decided to sow some grain. As he scattered the seed on the ground, some of it fell on a footpath and was trampled on, and the birds came and picked it off the hard ground and ate it"

"And some fell on rocky soil where there was little depth of earth; and the plants sprang up quickly enough in the shallow soil, but the hot sun soon scorched them and they withered and died, for they had no root."

"Other seeds fell among thorns that shot up and crowded the young plants so that they produced no grain."

"But some fell on good soil, and produced a crop that was thirty, sixty, and even a hundred times as much as he had planted. If you have ears, listen!"

What does this teaching of Jesus mean to you? How will it help you change? The grain is your ideas. In the first example is a person who places his grain on the hard path (negative path) that he has already traveled, and the birds are the negative forces that come in and snatch his hopes and dreams away.

The shallow, rocky soil represents a person who has heard the word of God, but for some reason doesn't take the message to heart. He knows the message is true and sort of believes it for a while, until trouble and persecution begin. Then his new-found belief wavers, and the negative thoughts dominate his mind once more.

The thorny ground represents the people who listen to the Word, receive it and believe it, but are choked out by the worry, stress and responsibilities of daily life.

The good soil represents the hearts of those who listen to the Word and hold onto it; they truly accept, go out and **use these ideas to produce true success and abundance.**

Just reading this book will not change your life. It won't help you until you **help yourself** by planting these ideas into the rich, positive soil of your soul. **Work on it daily,** protecting the seeds as they take root, not allowing the weeds of negativity to rob you of your passion. Once you **put these words into action** you will **discover an energy** that is impossible to describe. Once you feel this sensational surge of Positive Power you will never want to return to your old ways. But remember, you do have to **give it not only time, but effort** for at least thirty days. At that time, **evaluate the results**. If you **feel better** (and I'm positive you will) then you should **continue practicing and improving every day**. If you don't see or **feel the difference**, then return to your old, negative habits. Believe me, it won't take long for them to return.

It is amazing how positive people feel. The excitement, energy and new ideas that will come into your mind are a small part of the unusual experience. This is one reason companies like Mary Kay and Amway have been so successful. They have formed their own energy base, which they use to keep everybody charged. They do a great job of motivating their people. They **realize the impact of Positive Power**, and you can also **discover the secret to success and happiness.**

You need to **understand the importance of sharing** your enthusiasm, energy and excitement with others. The secret of living is giving. The more energy you **give to others**, the more excited you will be. So, **spread the word** about the Positive Power of God. **Catch the world on fire. Relight that spark** inside every human being. **Help change the world** while you are changing.

The purpose of these words is to propel you to the top of your chosen field and find your true path in life whatever that may be. They are also designed to bring you back to life and see you possess much more than you thought – they will transform you from merely existing to living in enlightenment and power. I pray this book will motivate you to **continue re-creating, changing and moving toward your next challenge** with zeal and enthusiasm, wherever your next dream may lead.

"Faith without works is dead."

James 2:26

You Must Believe

"All things are possible to him that believeth"

Jesus Christ

To create the miracle of restoration you must believe. You must **believe in a supreme energy** force that many of us call God. You also must **believe in yourself** and your abilities. If you don't nobody else will. And finally, you must **believe in the power of positive thinking**. You must **know that Positive Power will work for you** if you **work with Positive Power**.

Many people are not successful because they don't have confidence in themselves. Without self-confidence you will picture yourself as not worthy to live your dreams. I discovered a good example of lack of self-confidence while working at our local county fair. Our company had a free bean-bag toss, where people were challenged to throw three bean bags at bottles sitting less than ten feet away. There were no tricks and the game was easy. Because it was a promotion, we wanted the person to win the free gift. If the contestant knocked off the three bottles, they won a prize.

Many adults wouldn't play the free game. They answered that "I can't do that" or "I'd look stupid" or "what if I don't hit any?". These kinds of responses about such a trivial game started me thinking about how these people would face a true challenge or problem.

By reading positive material, associating with positive people and trying to **live your life in a positive manner every day**, you will **acquire a more positive attitude** and better self-esteem. It will feel strange at first. The beginning is always the hardest. Just **start working toward being a positive, loving person** and you will become what you focus on. Keeping a journal is a good way to start. Later, it is nice to be able to look back and **see how far you have advanced**. Each day, **find something you did right,** even if everything seemed like a failure. No matter how small the positive act, it is a start. If nothing else, write down that you had the courage to **start something new.** See how easy it is to **find something good to say** about yourself, instead of something mean and nasty.

Words are powerful, and these supposedly innocent verbal sounds can destroy or build a human being. The difference is the choice of words that are used, and how they are spoken.

A friend of mine was telling me about his mother, who had been severely ill. The doctors had informed him that his mother would be lucky if she lived another month. The son warned these medical experts that if they told her about the "death sentence" they had prescribed for her, he would sue them. My friend stayed with his mother twenty=four hours per day to make sure nobody would place any negative news into her mind. He understood the power of words.

This incident happened five years ago. His mother recovered and is still living a vibrant life. Who knows what might have happened, but this man believed so strongly in positive programming, and in the destructive power of negative words, that he did something that might have saved her life. I don't think we understand how powerful suggestion really is. The mind is like a computer, and we have to be careful what other people are programming into ours. We should **be more aware** of what we believe. All of what we think is true (beliefs) comes from our previous programming (words and experiences).

The mind is a terrible thing to waste. Too many of us turn our minds into a wasteland, filled with negative, toxic material. Like all garbage, it starts rotting. This is how a person gets 'stinking thinking'. If you don't want to propel negative vibes and toxic waste into society, you can't load your computer with negative input.

You have probably heard 'what goes in is what comes out' or 'you are what you eat'. Both of these truths can be useful in learning how to **live a positive, energized lifestyle**. If you **allow only positive thoughts into your mind** you will **produce positive output** when you really need it – when the times get tough.

Going through the tough times is hard, but it doesn't have to be difficult, especially if you know that God walks with you every step of the way. **Realize that everything happens for a purpose**, and you are never tempted by something you cannot surpass. **Watch for the opportunity to use the Positive Power of God in every situation**. It will never let you down. By understanding there is a lesson in every challenge, you will not allow the negative thinking to creep into your mind. I know Positive Power will win. I have bet my life on following the chosen path of

Jesus Christ. It is as effective today as it was two thousand years ago.

The righteous or "right thinking" path of life is the one far less traveled. Unlike the negative path that has been trampled wide, the Christ-like approach is narrow and has unlimited, hidden, negative traps designed to spring on you as you're attempting to travel on the straight and narrow journey. Even after you have chosen the positive way, there will always be forks in the road where the negative force will rear its ugly head. It takes courage to **make a stand** and **continue through these challenges**. When these difficult temptations face you, **ask yourself 'what would Jesus do?'** as well as which decision takes you closer toward your ultimate destination – Christ-consciousness.

Taking the positive path is not always the easiest, but it is the one that will make you **feel the best inside**. I admit that with all my years of walking with the white vibration of Positive Power, I still get caught in a negative state once in a while. Believe me, I have as many business, financial and personal situations as anybody else, but I have pre-chosen my destiny. I know in my heart that the Positive Power of

God will pull me through my daily challenges and advance me toward my next endeavor, as long as I keep the faith.

Most people, placed in hard times, will revert to a negative reaction. They know the positive words are true, but they don't have the willpower to withstand the dark side of negativity. I'm never sure why they think that this change to destructive thinking is going to help them get to where they want to be. Negativity never accomplishes anything. When a person takes on this poor attitude, it not only makes them poor in spirit, but they also cheat themselves out of the abundance of living and loving the moment.

These non-believers know better. At one time they believed. But, being positive in a difficult situation that takes discipline and faith. They start imagining negative pictures in their minds and jump off the positive bandwagon onto the negative ship that is going nowhere. This usually happens because they gave themselves to a predetermined amount of time for Positive Power to work. If they don't have what they expect by a certain date, then they declare that a positive belief system doesn't work and they return to the destructive side.

The truth is, these people can't face the challenge of digging deeper and having the discipline to continue through thick and thin. They make the mistake of *expecting* instead of *experiencing*. Don't expect. If you put expectation in your mind, you are setting yourself up for failure. Goals and dreams are to be worked toward. Not all of them will be achieved exactly when you want. The real excitement should be the daily challenge. That is what will keep you alive. When the reward arrives, and it will if you continue the program, it will be a blessing that you will cherish. Anything worth doing is worth waiting for. The longer it takes to manifest, the better it will be when you accomplish it.

****

Why are people so negative? Why can't they believe? Why can't they understand that it would be a better place for all of us if we all lived in harmony? Harmony is created by producing positive vibrations toward all other people, things and events. I remember when my wife and I were going through some very challenging times. We were walking down the beach at Venice Beach, California when

I saw an elderly gentleman giving massages. My body was so uptight I realized I needed to relax and asked if he could do one for me. I didn't realize I was going to get much more than just a massage.

The wise man counseled me in the financial, business and personal problems that I was experiencing. He seemed like he had known me my whole life, when in actuality he had met me only ten minutes prior. When Ann joined us, he said something neither one of us will ever forget. In his easy-going style, he shared these words: "**Relax.** Take it easy. Be kind to each other. We're all on this earth trying to do the best we can. And always remember, we're all in this bowl of soup together.".

This statement is so true, and to truly **live a perfect life** we must **eliminate our fear**, **anger**, **hate**, jealousy, killing, robbery, adultery. And anybody can **start changing** by simply making the decision to change.

I understand it is much easier to stay negative. All of us have felt "what's the use; why not just give up?" on the outside. But deep down inside, you know that you **believe in yourself** more than that. You just have to **change some habits**, and you will be on the road to recovery. Most of us have been programmed in a negative mode of thinking since childhood. We were told how we were bad, or weren't enough, how we failed, were too loud, or wasted our time dreaming. So, as you can see, for many of you, thinking negatively has been a habit for many years. The good news is that habits can be changed.

Another reason some people are negative and depressed about life is that something hasn't worked out for them the way that they thought it should have manifested. Most of us have dreamed, planned and hoped for riches, happiness, and financial success only to see our dreams slip through our fingers. Every time a disappointment hits us we have a tendency to become more depressed and start slowing down, not understanding that the past doesn't equal our future.

Many times, we start blaming God for these misfortunes, but God is love. God is not a person who is trying to make you miserable. Have you ever thought that maybe something happened because of your lack of faith in God? Without the protection of the divine Spirit, we're opening ourselves up to disaster from the dark side. God doesn't do things to us – man does. When another human being does an evil deed, s/

he is breaking God's commandments. S/he is not obeying the natural laws of mankind. This choice is made with the absence of positive and loving direction. That decision was formed by negative thoughts created by some form of fear and anger, not love.

You can give up and blame God. It's an easy escape, but never a pleasant journey. It's always your decision, but don't quit. Do yourself a favor and never let the prince of darkness be your king. If you quit dreaming, you quit living. When you quit living, the light of God is hidden and your world becomes a black hole.

Every one of us has setbacks and disappointments. We have to **expect these obstacles** if we **plan on moving ahead**. I have personally experienced thousands of disappointments, but because I **understand that everything that happens to us can be a lesson. I find the strength to keep plunging ahead.** I **don't blame God** for the problem. I **thank Him.** I understand that He will never confront me with a challenge I can't handle. I also know that He will give me the strength and the tools to conquer this part of my quest and move on to the next hurdle.

"Why," you may ask, "do I want to put myself through a lifetime of disappointment and frustration?" The answer is that if you give up, you force yourself into a void with no reason. All of us need a reason to get up every morning, **stay excited** and **be striving toward something more purposeful** than just working for a weekly paycheck to pay the bills and survive. I'm referring to a reason to really be living. There is something bigger and better for each one of us, and that is living the dream that God has given us. That is the purpose of living – a reason. The purpose of life is to **live with purpose.**

Successful people know this reason – this burning desire. Some refer to it as "the eye of the tiger". These excited individuals have had as many failures and probably more than most negative people. But the difference is how they pictured failure. They **perceive it as a learning experience**. They **understand that to become successful you must have experience**. To have experience you must **try**. When you try you might fail more times than not, which gives you the experience to **know how to succeed**. So, successful people **see failure not as a personal mistake**, **but rather a stepping stone** to happiness and success.

I confess to my audiences that I have failed more times than all of them combined. Of course, they don't believe me, and they are shocked to hear this true evaluation of my life. They sit there wondering why they're listening to me, but then quickly learn my secret. They discover that nobody is above failure. I've done the things that I've accomplished because I am no longer scared of failure. I have learned how to take its ugly face and make a friend. How do I do it?

It's easy. I **take one step at a time** toward my goal. I make up my mind that this particular obstacle is not going to be the one failure to stop me from achieving my dream and living the life I desire. I will not let failure win. I **use failure**. I will use it however I can, however I need to use it. The most important thing is that I will not let it defeat me. I will not quit. I hope you feel the same way. **Use this one empowering idea** and you will **get farther than you ever imagined.**

Failure is not the almighty end unless you believe it is and quit. If you **don't bow down and submit to this negative energy, keep moving ahead, learn from the misfortune,** and **adjust your game plan**, you will **be more successful** because of it. I know this sounds easy. Meanwhile, your mind is crying out for help because you're drowning in frustration. Sometimes it's hard to **see the light**, but there is hope on the horizon. If you don't have hope, what do you have to believe in?

"This is the day the Lord has made; let us **rejoice** and **be glad** in it."

Psalm 118:24

Don't Give Up – Get Up!

*"Do not be afraid, **stand firm** and see the deliverance that the Lord will accomplish for you today."*

Exodus 14:13

At a certain age, too many people give up – they give in. They lose their zest for life, that twinkle in their eye, settling for what life will give them instead of going out and getting what they want. You don't just want to settle for the scraps when you can have a feast, do you?

Do you believe that your goals are too hard to achieve, or that you can't reach your dreams? If you have this thinking, then **change your thinking** or change your goals. Don't set yourself up for failure. You can **accomplish what your dream is** if you **set reasonable goals, work hard, work smart,** and **never give up.** And even if a dreamer doesn't reach the star s/he is trying to touch, are they not closer than if they had never tried?

What star do you want to touch? Whatever you want to do, you must **believe with all your heart, soul and mind**

that you can accomplish the task. Until you **believe you can**, you won't do it – guaranteed.

One of my goals in hairdressing was to work for the Nexxus haircare company – a giant in the professional haircare market. I had met the founder, Mr. Jerri Redding, in 1980. At that time I was a young hairdresser who had a sick baby daughter - Leslie, who was suffering from convulsions. Ann and I had upset our medical doctor, refusing to put our baby on potentially harmful drugs. Trying everything, we prayed for a miracle by asking Mr. Redding, who was a nutritionist and herbalist, if he could help us. Believe it or not, without seeing her and only hearing her symptoms, he diagnosed her with an allergy to milk. He suggested a milk substitute and a B-complex vitamin. She never had another convulsion.

If we hadn't stood firm on what we believed, we would have fallen for what the "experts" had told us. Our daughter could be a vegetable today. Our goal was to save our daughter's life. We had one purpose, believed there was an answer, and refused to give up. We wouldn't quit when everybody told us we were harming her by not listening to the doctors. We didn't give in when the welfare department was called in to check if we were reliable parents. And because we didn't quit, knew our outcome, and believed, with Mr. Redding's help, our Leslie is now a healthy, grown woman. Thank God we listened to our inner voice and had the faith to follow it.

Because of Mr. Redding's help, I promised I would work for his company as a platform artist and educator. Being from a small town in the Midwest, everybody explained to me why I couldn't realize my dream of working for this west coast company. But I listened to myself instead of being influenced by the negative doomsayers. For twelve years, I passionately dreamed every night my vision that I was featured as a national stylist from the Midwest Beauty Show in Chicago. My dream manifested when I was selected as one of five hairdressers (the only one from the Midwest) to be a member of the first National Nexxus Tour in 1992 – twelve years after the original vision was given to me.

Don't give up – get up! Get up right now out of the rut and **do something** about whatever the problem is. **Do it right now.** Put this book down and make that phone call, write that letter, or whatever it is going to take to get the ball rolling. It is time to get started. It takes most people twenty years to become truly successful, yet most people give up long before this double decade. By doing something toward your goal NOW, you are one step closer to making your dream a reality.

Congratulations for reading this far. You haven't given up. You **believe this information can help you**, and you are looking for assistance to make your journey more pleasant. Hopefully by now you have some ideas or direction you need to travel. Don't question the path you've selected. You will never go wrong if you **take direction from your inner voice** which is your soul talking to you.

Don't hesitate. Take action. Who in their right mind would start down a certain trail, only to stop in the middle of the journey and question where they were – unless they were lost? Are you still lost? Are you afraid to get started? If you don't **make a decision** and stick to it, you will find yourself going around in circles and not getting anywhere. Have you ever felt that way?

I hope by now these words have rekindled the God-spark that burns deep inside you. It's too easy to get unmotivated and stuck. I know; it happened to me. For years I was the most motivated person around. People would comment on how energetic and positive I was every day. I was proud of my positive attitude, and then it happened – the negativity bug attacked me. It can happen to anyone, and it does happen to most people at some point in life – even the most motivated ones.

I can attest that you can **change**. You don't have to give up. You can get back up and **try** again. I did. It is not what has happened or what we have done in the past. The important thing is how we feel and what we accomplish today and tomorrow. After losing my positive attitude, but not my dreams, I rescued myself out of self-pity, laziness and negative thinking, and got back to the attitude that saved my life, and the one I practice every day – the Positive Power of God!

Change is difficult. It is work, but it can be fun. It's like swimming upstream or walking the opposite way on a busy sidewalk. It is always easier, with less stress and friction, to go in the same direction as the crowd – negative and unhappy. Remember, to get the "buck" to flow (and find true happiness) you have to buck the flow.

Many people are unhappy because they have given up on life. Look around. You know who I'm talking about. They have given up the fight for what they dreamed and deserved, satisfied with the crumbs that have been given them. These people secretly know inside themselves that they could have done better, but they didn't do it because of one excuse or another. Don't give me an excuse. Give me a result. Don't give yourself excuses. **Show the world that you can do it.**

I was talking recently to a single mother of two young boys. She was struggling, trying not to go on welfare. Her ex-husband was not paying child support. She was having a very difficult time. But what impressed me about this girl was that she still had a dream. She had a dream of opening up her own beauty salon, but her family was against it. They were trying to force her to work in a factory. "That would kill my spirit," she confessed.

This woman knew the true secret of life – pursuing a dream. Too many of us get trapped believing that happiness is things that we gather on our journey, such as cars, houses, clothes, money and trinkets. They protect these things with their life, literally. They give up their life to hold onto these things. They work jobs they hate, to keep or get these things. They would not think about sacrificing any of these things to live in true success. Yet, the truth is that you can't steal second and keep your foot on first. Sometimes you have to **take a calculated risk to live your dream life**.

What is your situation now, and how do you view it? I was talking to a businessman about turning forty. I asked him how his life was going. He informed me he was very satisfied with his life and didn't have anything else he wanted to do. I thought to myself how strange I must be because as successful as I was, I was not completely satisfied. I had a great family, and had accomplished many of my goals, but that shouldn't mean I had to be satisfied with my performance on earth. I knew I had much more to do. I knew my mission in life had not been fulfilled. I had a destiny for greatness.

Do you **feel a burning desire inside to do more**, **be more** and **have more**? Do you ever ask yourself why you are here? We all have these questions in our minds at one time or another. If you bury these feelings, like so many people do, because of other commitments, fear, or laziness, you will never be completely satisfied. There will always be this nagging feeling in the back of your mind that will keep saying over and over – I could have, should have, would have....but.

There is a word that describes a person who tries to be something or someone, but because of one excuse or another they can't make the grade - "wannabe". These poor souls 'want to be' but never seem to realize their dreams. Don't be a "wannabe". **Be what you want to** be.

Many people say, "okay, I'll try." I tell them, don't try – do. There is no such thing as trying. There is either doing it or not doing it. There is no gray area. You are putting action toward your goals and dreams or you're not. It's that simple. The question is; are you working toward your dreams or are you still only "trying"?

If you give up, you lose the magic of life where there is always a possibility of something great happening. If you don't **get up right now** and say that you're going to give it another shot, you'll never know whether your dream really can be a reality.

Imagine. Just think what a person with imagination, belief and determination can accomplish. This type of person doesn't give up because something doesn't go the way they wanted. Since these people know the outcome already, they just keep working on it until they get the outcome they have envisioned. Thomas Edison was once asked by a young reporter how he felt about failing 1,000 times trying to invent the electric lightbulb. He commented, "young man, I have not failed 1,000 times trying to invent the electric lightbulb. Rather, I have successfully shown 1,000 ways the electric lightbulb will not work."

You can be this type of person. You can **be a magician** and **make your life magical**. Remember, what the mind of man can conceive and believe he can achieve. What can your imagination conceive? Can you **believe it**? With determination and persistence you can achieve it.

Are you a creative thinker - a problem-solver? If you are, then you're on your way to success. Instead of giving up, **look at your problems as opportunities** and challenges to **use your creative abilities**.

Imagination is a wonderful thing. It's something we have as children but lose as we grow through the knocks of life. Trying to be creative might have been dismissed as daydreaming or wasting your time. Many of us were trained to ignore our creative side, yet this is the power that you need right now to **awaken the giant within you.** For some reason, in today's world creativity is looked at as a curse, rather than a blessing. Too many people would rather not have to think or use their imagination. Instead, they suffer through the reality of working another boring day, rather than letting their minds create the freedom for which they are secretly searching.

Don't stop your creative thinking. Use it or you'll lose it. Take a moment; sit back; close your eyes and let your mind relax. Push the daily woes from your mind and let new creative energy flow into it. You are a creative person in many ways. You might not realize it, but you are.

Think about your life now. When you really want something, you do know how to get it, don't you? You're using your imagination and creativity when you approach another person for a date, look for a new job, or do that project around the house. Yet, too many people refuse to use this God-given gift when they are designing their lives.

Imagination is the beginning of every idea that has ever been accomplished. Every convenience you now use started as an idea. Once the idea is formed and you have visualized the completed image, you can reach your goal of turning the thought and vision into reality. Without imagination, nothing could go through this natural process of invention. It's not time for you to "invent" the perfect life for you.

How can you use imagination at work, at home, in your relationship, or to reach your goals? Creative thinking is an asset that will be valuable to recreate your life and achieve resurrection of your life. What would be the perfect job, the perfect day, the perfect place to live, the perfect mate, the perfect minute? With imagination and Positive Power, you can achieve these aspects of life.

One reason many of you cannot be creative is that you are stressed. You can't be stressed out and get your creative energy to flow. Worrying about money, work, health, relationships, children, and other problems kills your creativity. The best advice I can give to you that I use is "let go, let God". If you will put your life in the hands of the Ultimate Power, you don't have to worry. Then you can concentrate on more empowering things.

The more uptight you are, the less you'll be able to open up and release your creative energy, which is how you're going to find the answer to your new life. It will take all the energy you have for you to reach the top. This creative energy is only released when you're not doubting yourself, but believing it can happen. By "buying" into yourself and your ideas, you will have the confidence, motivation and direction to move on your dreams. That's what I call creative energy. Positive Power is the ability to act in a positive way. That is what you are doing when you follow these steps, which are guaranteed to get you closer to your dream and goals.

What is worrying you? What is stopping you from living the perfect life? Are you too busy trying to earn a living to have time to design a life? I was there for a long time also. If you don't watch it, you will get into a rut of life – a comfort zone – safe, comfortable and easy. Sure, you want more but...

Most of you have yourselves fixed into "cracking the monthly nut". Many people have the income budgeted to the dollar on what can be spent when and on what. We get caught up in this monthly cycle of working to pay the bills, only to have very little of it left over – if we're lucky. Yet, many fall prey to this situation. Is this the way that you really want to live? Is this how you want your family to live?

So many people think that this is security. They might get ahead a little, and they are scared to take chances. But life is funny. Just when you think you are comfortable, life kicks you in the butt. It's true. Look at what happened to us. We owned three businesses, and because of uncontrolled situations, bad management decisions, and over-expansion, they all three failed. Because we were relying on these businesses for our income, we went from being well-off to having nothing. We tell people today that it was like jumping off of a cliff, flapping our wings and not knowing whether we were going to land or crash. We were scared, but positive that this change of events was for a bigger purpose, and that God knew what He was doing – and He did.

If these businesses had not closed I would still be riding the comfort tide through life, never being pushed to grow. We were making a decent living. It was so decent I had to let myself get stuck in a comfortable lifestyle.

How do you know when you're stuck? It's easy. Have you ever been stuck in a hole? You can feel it. You feel uncomfortable, under stress, and nervous. You know you have to do something to get unstuck.

If you get stuck in the rut of life, you have a choice. Remember, when you're green you grow, and when you're ripe you rot. If you feel you are rotting you have the choice to change. Too many people feel trapped like a rat, concerned with their family responsibilities. They get tired. These unhappy souls start wearing down after putting hours and hours into a living they know is not what they are supposed to be accomplishing. They feel as if they are being forced – as if life has cheated them. That isn't true. Life has nothing to do with it. They are cheating themselves. They are the ones who have made the choices and are still making those choices.

If you feel like you are in this situation, know right now that you can **start making positive choices** that will give you a better life, but it won't be easy. There is no free lunch. Everybody wants out of the rut but not everyone wants to invest the energy, time or money. So, instead of getting up they give up. Most use the "victim" excuse – how they don't have the money or time. They explain that when they get the money or have the time, they will change.

These people have it backwards, and when you live life backwards it spells E-V-I-L. You have to **commit to**

a change and apply every ounce of creative energy and action toward your desired outcome before the big payoff is going to happen.

I ask my students "have you ever seen a farmer harvest a field?" Most of them answer yes, until I ask the second part of the question - "before he plants and works the field?" Of course the students understand this would be impossible, yet they expect a harvest of money before they break the soil, plant, weed, fertilize, and finally harvest. We should all learn from the farmer.

So **don't give up, get up** and **do something**. Break up the soil; **plant the seeds**; pull out the weeds and **grow your ideas. Take action.** But to do this you must **believe in yourself.** You're the only one who knows your destiny. You **imagine it in your head.** You **dream about it all the time.** It won't go away. You're confident it will work. The only problem is... you still don't know if **you can do it.**

Even with everything I have told you up to this point, many of you have still not taken action. Why? It comes down to one word – fear.

"Whatsoever you do, work at it with all your heart, as working for the Lord, not for men... It is the Lord Christ you are serving."

Colossians 3:23, 24

Turning Fear Into Power

"God hath not given us the spirit of fear, but of power and love and of a sound mind."

2 Timothy 1:7

Talking about fear isn't easy. Most of us don't want to admit that we are scared to death of something, but the real truth is we do let fear stop us. Do you have everything you want? Have you done everything you ever wanted to do, gone everywhere you have ever desired to go? If you said "no" to these questions – and who could say yes, then fear is stopping you.

Fear isn't necessarily an enemy. The emotion of fear can be good. It is designed to protect us, which is demonstrated in the fight-or-flight instinct that we all possess. Fear starts extra adrenaline flowing through our bodies to produce extra energy and speed to escape a predator or fight an intruder.

But to many people, fear is not a friend. It is a foe. They feel the nervousness as they envision negative pictures in their minds. This type of fear paralyzes people from taking the necessary action to become happy and successful. When this is the result of fear, it is a detriment.

So, as we see, fear is based on how each individual perceives it. To some, the nervousness from the adrenaline rush is a signal to be scared and worry. For others, including myself, this rush is what we live for. Everything else is just waiting. As I am waiting to go onstage to speak, I am always nervous. The minute I am scheduled to step on stage I feel a tremendous rush of adrenaline. But once on stage, the nervousness is transformed into energy that I share with my audience. By expanding this unique energy of positive vibration, I am able to excite thousands of people. If I viewed this signal of fear in the negative way, I would never step onstage.

Fear is an emotion, and all emotions can be used in a positive way. Fear is only as powerful as we allow it to be. Remember the acronym of FEAR is **F**alse **E**vidence **A**ppearing **R**eal. In other words, when you fear something, it has usually not happened yet. So what you are doing is picturing what you expect to happen, and you are visualizing it in a negative manner. If you perceived the same situation with a positive result, then you wouldn't fear it. Right?

Why do most people fear the unknown? Why do so many people picture future events in a negative darkness?

The warden at the high-security prison always talked to the prisoner sentenced to death on the day of his execution. He always gave them the same speech: "I like to give each prisoner a fair chance, so I am letting you choose your own fate. You can select the firing squad that is waiting for you outside, or you may walk through that black door." He pointed to the closed dark door on the other side of the room. The convict, not hesitating, pointed out the window. "I want to see who is executing me. I choose the firing squad." The warden asked the prisoner one more time if he was sure, and it was confirmed. The man was placed in front of the seven guns pointing straight at him and in one loud noise he fell to the ground. The warden looked down at the dying man. Their eyes met and as a last request the prisoner asked "warden I just gotta know before I die. What was behind the black door?" In his last breath he heard the words that he so longed to hear: "Freedom, my son, freedom".

Are you letting a "black door" stop you from personal freedom? Are you punishing yourself because of the fear of facing the unknown? Do you fear an upcoming event because you see it as a negative? Aristotle once said, "Fear is pain brought on by the anticipation of evil." If you are painting a false image in your mind, you need to change that picture right now!

What you must understand is that the world is not how you or I personally see it. We view everything through our own personally designed glasses. These lenses have been affected by our mental programming, which we have been receiving since birth.

This mental programming is a recording of our complete life. Every word, action, sound, movement and thought is contained in these files. This recorded history is the basis of all future perception, which is always changing.

All of us are what I like to refer to as "human becomings". All humans are *becoming* either more positive or more negative in their perception of the world. Becoming more negative is the path of least resistance. It takes no extra energy or effort to fall into a darkened state. The mind is like a garden – it must be worked with to keep the weeds of negativity out of the fertile soil. It doesn't take work to grow weeds. It takes effort to possess a positive attitude. It is natural for the body to gravitate toward the lower vibration of negativity.

If we have had a positive upbringing then we won't fear as much because we'll see our world in a more positive way. But if we have been raised in a negative environment, our pictures will be distorted, with negative results. It's like taking pictures of a beautiful landscape with the camera out of focus. How good will the picture be? How truly will the snapshot capture the real moment? The camera can only take as good a picture as the lens has focused. Our daily lives work like this. Two people can look at the same situation and see two totally different outcomes. (Remember the two shoe salesmen?)

Fear is a major obstacle stopping people from living the life that God has given them to fulfill. Fear is lack of trust in God. You cannot **attempt great things** and let fear stop you. I'm not saying there won't be fear. But, what I am stating is that to be great you must **acknowledge that fear is there** and then **break through the perceived fear and conquer it.**

Our fire walk is an excellent example of showing how a person can turn fear into power. At the seminar, the attendees in the beginning are very apprehensive about walking barefoot on red-hot coals. There is fear in their minds because they picture burning their feet. They let disempowering images creep into their minds. But by the conclusion of the program, when it is time to perform the actual walk, every person is able to face the fear, put themselves in an empowered state and **prove that fear can be conquered.**

Once you **conquer fear** and imagined impossibility, the question becomes "what other fear can you conquer?" This fire walk exercise opens up other possibilities that many of the participants had never thought were possible. What bed of hot coals do you need to walk? What fear do you need to face?

Fear stops you from living your dreams. That's all – just fear. Isn't it terrible that this small four-letter-word has so much power over us? But it does. The biggest fear is fear itself. If we can take this emotion and learn how to take its intensity away, then fear will not be as big a factor in our quest to be our best.

How do you do that? Action! Action eliminates fear. Think back and remember something you were scared of doing but which you finally achieved. Are you scared of doing it now? Probably not, or at least not as scared as the first time. If you can get yourself to **take action** you can break the fear cycle. Once you successfully loosen this grip that fear has on you, you can **claim your freedom**.

It takes guts. It takes courage. And the great news iss you don't have to do it alone. All you have to do is ask for guidance and believe, and the power of God will be with you every step of the way. It won't be easy the first time. Do whatever it is you need to do to get your dream moving toward reality. Confront that person whom you feel uneasy being around, though you need his or her help. A good approach to finding the courage is to ask yourself the following questions: What's the worst thing that could happen if I attempted this goal? Can I handle the worst?

If you can handle the worst that could possibly happen, then why not **go for the gold**? Why not **think big**? Whatever you are dreaming won't be as difficult as you have pictured. **Just do it.** That is the well-known, but seldom-recognized secret, isn't it?

I remember procrastinating about starting my personal coaching business. Like many, I had pictures in my mind that were slowing me down from achieving my dream. Reading a local newspaper, I noticed an advertisement for another personal development coach. I immediately called her. The one question I asked during our conversation was how she had started her business. Her answer was so simple, yet painstakingly truthful - "I just made up mind I wanted to do it, and I did!"

Imagine for a moment if achieving your dream was really as easy as "just doing it". Sounds too easy doesn't it? Well, in a certain way it is that easy. No, I'm not telling you that one step of action is going to give you your ultimate desire, but it will start you toward your dream. If you will **take action immediately** toward what you sincerely believe in, ardently desire, and **never give up on**, you can achieve your wildest dreams.

By understanding, believing and living by these and other words of empowerment you will live a life full of vitality and energy. The reason so many people are living a dead life is because they don't understand or believe in The Great Lifestyle. The secret of resurrection is to **discover**

your dreams again and believe that they are possible through the power of God.

One approach you should remember is; if somebody else has already accomplished it, then you can do it. A good example is the four-minute mile. Before Roger Bannister accomplished breaking this perceived impossible barrier, everybody believed it was humanly impossible. Experts agreed that the body could not withstand such torture. It was impossible – until Roger Bannister proved them wrong by doing the "impossible". Once he accomplished this "impossible" feat, many other runners were able to do it as well.

When the group of fire walk hopefuls were standing around the hot embers, I saw fear on their faces. So to break this fear I walked across first to show them it is possible. As soon as they witnessed me accomplishing "the impossible" they believed they could do it also. They followed my lead and literally stepped through their fear.

If you worry that you can't accomplish your dream find somebody who has already accomplished it. Knowing they accomplished your dream should give you the confidence to **attempt what you want to achieve**.

Fear is one of the largest epidemics in the United States today. It stops more people from living their dream than any other factor. Fear is success's major roadblock. It is a powerful force. It is a psychological dis-ease. It is a mind-virus. This emotion is fabricated in the mind and is usually not real. But because it is the figment of your negative imagination, you can easily **change it**.

Fear is a disempowering state that affects your life by stopping you from doing what you want to do. Walt Disney asked the famous question: "What would you do if you knew you could not fail?" When I ask audiences this question, most people don't have a problem writing down a list of things they would do if they knew there was no possible failure. Yet, they haven't lived their dreams because, whether consciously or unconsciously, they feared failure.

To **become alive again**, you must not let fear **control your life**. Remember: "If you aren't doing what you want to do, there is no doubt fear has conquered you." **Don't let fear conquer you. Don't let it become the barrier to your success**. Don't let it rear its ugly head and scare you into submitting to its false power, keeping you in your own self-imposed prison.

To **conquer fear,** you must **have the courage to face fear** and **replace the feeling of fear with the feeling of excitement**. Yes, fear can be good. A new paradigm of fear is excitement. When fear is felt, the body automatically produces extra adrenaline. Your heart starts beating faster, your mind becomes more alert. It is preparing you for the challenge. Use that extra nervousness, which is energy, and put it to good use.

Erica Jong once stated, "Everyone has talent. What is rare is the courage to follow the talent to the dark place where it leads." Welcome fear as a friend, not as a foe. **Reframe the way you approach fear,** and it will not stop you.

Remember that everybody experiences fear. The successful people know how to use fear to their benefit in a constructive way. Unsuccessful people allow fear to stop them.

Learn how to reprogram fear so you can **turn fear into power.** You must **understand why you fear things.** You have been programmed since childhood to fear the unknown or everything that is new or outside your comfort zone. Fear is the outside wall of your comfort zone. Some of us have bigger comfort zones than others. This does not mean that one person is any better than another. What it does show is who has had more experiences in the world and has learned from them.

Anybody can **step through fear** if they want. **Remember that whenever you feel fear, it means you are stretching your comfort zone** – you are growing. Ray Kroc, the founder of McDonald's, once said "When you are green you grow and when you are ripe you rot". So, when you are fearing something new, it's because you are expanding and doing something new. Look at it as an opportunity to learn and live. And when you do this action and accomplish it, you will expand your comfort zone.

Every time you **face fear and take action despite fear,** which is courage, then you are making your comfort zone larger. The larger your comfort zone, the better life you will live. You won't have to live with fear as much. And the great part is that you can **keep growing your comfort zone** because each experience that you accomplish gives you more courage.

William Shakespeare expressed it in this fashion: "our doubts are traitors and make us lose the good we oft might win, by fearing to attempt."

An NLP (Neuro-Linguistic Programming) approach to handling fear is expressed in how you look at fear inside your mind. When people experience fear they usually "see" the situation through their own eyes. Because they experience this negative thought as if it were happening to them, the negative emotion of fear feels very real. This picturing process is called associative conditioning. This technique will give you the strongest feelings because it is as if you are personally experiencing the situation.

To decrease the intensity of fear, you must "dissociate" yourself from the fearful situation. In other words, instead of picturing it through your own eyes, take the time to view the situation ass a movie that you are in. Do not see it through your eyes, but rather watch yourself watching the movie. This exercise puts some distance between you and the fear. If you do this exercise, you will feel the fear less intensely.

There are many NLP techniques that we teach in our classes that will help anybody **learn to control fear** or phobias. There are many good books about this incredible technology if you want more information.

Another way to handle fear is to **act "as if"**. If you are scared of something, **picture in your mind how you would act if you were courageous**. I was talking to a new attorney who had hired me to help him through the fear of speaking in a courtroom. I asked him if he had ever been courageous, and as his body posture slumped he answered a meek "no". I then asked him if he knew somebody that he thought was courageous and this time he answered with a confident "yes".

I asked Bill why he thought this other person was courageous. He told me it was how the man presented himself. When I asked him how this person presented himself, Bill explained in detail what the other person looked like – the suit he was wearing. I continued by asking him what else told him this other person was courageous. My client explained how his hero spoke so confidently. Again, I questioned Bill on how the other person stood. Before we were done, I had Bill standing and speaking like the person he had modeled.

In NLP, the technique of Modeling is copying somebody's actions, words, gestures, tempo and tone of voice, to produce the same result. This is something that you can do. If you are having problems with fear, find someone who faces fear and deals with it and copy them. It will absolutely help you **turn your fear around**.

By using these techniques, you can **turn fear into power**. Fear is no more than a mental barrier stopping you from living the dreams that you would love to live. It is up to you to **welcome fear as a friend** not a foe, and you will have made another step on your journey of resurrecting your life.

To **take back your life** you have to find the courage to **face fear**. As many great scholars have stated in slightly different prose, the biggest fear is fear itself. You must **break through whatever it is that is stopping you**.

I was on a sales call with a trainer, and we were cold-calling on a large business. Joe, the East Coast mega sales star for the company, watched as I buckled under the pressure of fear. Believe me, I know the feeling. We lose our confidence, picturing a negative outcome. Joe picked up on my negative vibes immediately. "What's wrong with you? I've never seen you like this before."

"Nothing", I falsely claimed, not doing a very good job of hiding my feelings. "Bull. You're scared." Joe was right. It was a terrible feeling. Joe embarrassed me so much that his insulting comments became more painful than the previous picture that had been stuck in my mind. Without warning, I turned toward the door, walked up to it, shoved it open without knocking, looked the owner right in the eye and said "You have been putting me off for weeks. Your buddy Gary told me you were a nice guy and I'm not so sure about that!"

He stammered and tried to explain that he had been very busy, and I quickly hammered a day and time out of him. To make a long story short, I went back at the agreed time and he did buy from me. Would he have been a customer if I had not finally gotten so fed up with Joe's comments that I forgot about the pain of fear and went forward? Probably not.

What do I have to say to you to get you so mad that you will **discover that passion that is lying dormant in you?**

What is it going to take in your life to say "I've had it! I'm not going to take it anymore"?

Sad but true; it usually takes a drastic situation to make people change. As humans we are so scared of the unforeseen future that we would rather smother in the past. We base our lives from the viewpoint of what we've accomplished; how much money we've collected or the number of toys we've purchased. But we also live with "mistakes" we have made. We allow our negative emotions like guilt, fear, hate, jealousy, greed, lust and anger to weigh us down like anchors.

The truth is that your life has nothing to do with what you have done or not done. It is all about what you're doing NOW and what you are going to do with your God-given potential. Your slate will be cleaned as soon as you believe that it is. You **start over fresh the minute you choose.** There is nobody stopping you from resurrecting yourself into a new life this very second. In the blink of an eye you can **possess the passion that God intended for you to use in His name.**

Feel the pain. Know your feelings. Don't kill the messenger with drugs, alcohol and/or prescriptions.

These signals of negativity attacking God's temple are the only way you're going to know that you are alive. A person with no emotions is dead! Expressing your emotions is not bad. There is nothing wrong about a person crying. It is God-like to show your love. You can never love too much. Don't hold back what you are feeling. That is the real you. The only way to know yourself is to **allow your soul to tell you how it feels.** It will never lie to you.

"Because of your faith, you will **be heard**."

Matthew 9:29

<u>Modeling the Master</u>

"He that believeth in me, the works that I do shall he do also..."

John 14:12

The secret of success is not a secret. All you have to do is **decide exactly what you want** and then **go for it** with everything you have. **Become obsessed with your dream. Know your outcome,** and **pay the price**, whatever that price may be. This is exactly what Jesus taught by example. He was the perfect model two thousand years ago, and still is today.

To **live life to its fullest** you must **refuse anything but your best**. The raising of your standards will **change the quality of your life**. With a model like Jesus to copy, you will **do it better than you ever dreamed possible**. By using modeling, you can **learn in minutes what it takes others years to learn**. To **live your dream, be excited about living** and being resurrected requires effort and effective action so you will **see results.**

Results cause excitement and enthusiasm. That's what you need as soon as possible. If these words inspire you to **try something** you've always wanted to do, but because of no experience you fail too many times you will lose the confidence to **continue**. With a mentor you will be able to avoid many obstacles and **learn the secrets of success and happiness**.

Modeling saves the most precious commodity – time. If you sow the same seed you will reap the same rewards. Why try to reinvent the wheel? There are certain patterns of thoughts and actions that bring success and other habits that bring failure. You are where you are because of these patterns. If you don't like where your thoughts and actions have gotten you, then you must **change** to **come back to life** and **live again!** And all you have to do is **find a role model** and **copy his/her actions.**

What would you like to change about yourself? Why did you "die" in the first place? Did you "fail" at something? Did you give up on your dream? Most human beings are looking for change. The quickest way to accomplish whatever you desire to do is to find someone who has already demonstrated it and model that person to the best of your ability.

What actions did these people take? What do they think? How do they do what they do? Find out these facts. **Become a detective** and **look for these clues to success. Ask lots of questions** and **observe their actions.** Ask yourself, "how does s(he) **create that result?** If you do this you will **produce outstanding results** in a short period of time.

The person whom you select to model does not have to be alive. If it is someone who is deceased, then **imagine what they would do**, knowing their background and accomplishments. If you don't know how they acted about something, **ask yourself how you imagine them acting** and **use that as your model.**

When you **learn how to model** you are learning the process of duplicating excellence, which will produce outstanding results. It does not make a bit of difference what has happened to you in the past. The past does not equal the future. What does matter is for you to **seize the day** and **have the discipline to learn from the professionals.**

I was talking to a business associate at a recent luncheon, and the conversation went like this: "Jerry, how do you always get along with everybody? You never meet a stranger."

"I model my mentor."

"Do you mind if I ask who's your mentor? I'd like to learn from him."

"Jesus Christ is my model" I proudly declared. "I teach the Positive Power of God through the teachings of Jesus Christ. You're a Christian, aren't you?"

"Praise the Lord" my friend chanted, as he showed me his well-worn W.W.J.D. bracelet, hidden under his long-sleeve white dress shirt and business suit. "You know what this means, don't you?"

"Doesn't everybody? The real question is how many people really **live the life that Jesus lived, think the thoughts that He thought; treat people the way that He treated them?** By the way, I didn't even know you were wearing one of those bracelets."

"There's lots of people who wear the W.W.J.D. bracelets, shirts, and jewelry. I just have to keep mine covered while I'm working company policy...you know."

"You're covering up Jesus?! And you feel good about that?"

"Rules are rules. And you know, Jerry, a man has to do what a man has to do to make a living. I'm fourty-years old. I have one kid in college and another one close. I make good money. I'm not going to rock the boat."

I looked at my friend and asked him one last question; "what *would* Jesus do, *really?*"

I applaud every person who truly asks them self the question "what would Jesus really do?" and then do it. It is not about wearing something. To model, you must be. There is no trying to **model Jesus Christ**. You are, or you're not. If you **make a positive, loving choice** you are following Jesus. If you make a decision that has negative emotions connected to it, you are not modeling Jesus. **Remember what He told us** - "Follow me".

As you travel through your daily journey you need to **become more aware of what Jesus would do.** Don't be like my friend above that thought he couldn't change. Using Jesus or any enlightened human being as your model will place you on the correct path of finding peace of mind and true success. By following their words and duplicating their actions, you will **resurrect yourself to the most high** – serving your fellow human being in a positive way.

This is the answer to how I **get along with everybody**. I treat every person like I believe Jesus would treat them. To **live the life of this master**, you must not only like other people, you must communicate with all of them with kindness, love and compassion on a positive energy level.

When talking to people, **do more than talk. Listen. Listen for their need. Heal them by lending an ear and listening.** God did give us two ears and one mouth. Maybe He was trying to tell us that we should **listen twice as much as we talk.**

Jesus knew His purpose and He understood that to accomplish His mission He would have to have help from other people. To really live your dreams, you're going to have to **have other people help you.** Whatever you want to accomplish, you will need the help of someone else. By starting right now to **understand the importance of human relations**, you are preparing yourself to **really live.**

To **change your life,** you have to interreact with other people. You will need to take chances of them rejecting you, if you really want to live. The situation with people who are sleepwalking through life, is they are buried in a tight, safe cocoon and won't dare come outside their cozy area.

But, like water that is stagnant, the person becomes stale. Like muscles that don't get used, atrophy destroys their self-esteem, people skills and motivation. Most of these society hermits have a negative image about other people, not understanding the same negative image is staring back at them in the mirror.

Because of this negative perception of people, they refuse to **communicate with others**. These skeptics don't **trust others** because they have been hurt in the past. The social offender commits a devastating crime against their future. They put 'all of them in the same basket'. They mistakenly don't realize that every individual person is a human becoming. Every person is unique. Some are bad, others are wonderful. And you can't possibly know until you **get to know them**.

I understand that some of you are screaming "I can't believe that Dr. Weber is telling us to **talk to strangers!**" That is exactly what I'm saying. On the other hand, I'm also as earnestly cautioning to **use good judgement**. But, **judge ye not.**

Who was the last person that you said "hello" to that you didn't know? I remember a lady who I was standing in line with that I greeted. She looked at me strangely and asked "Do I know you?" I confirmed her confusion with "no". Acting frustrated because a stranger had spoken to her, she quipped 'then why did you say hello to me?'

I smiled and replied "because we're in the same race". Now I had her really confused but intrigued.

"What race?"

Knowing I had already won the challenge I humbly answered, "the human race."

Many people refer to life as a "rat race". I don't understand why any human would continue working so hard to win a rat race. Even if you win, you're still a rat. But, if you are living as if you are in the human race, and you win, then you are a compassionate, loving human being.

To **restore life** and **be resurrected** out of the grave of yesterday's beliefs, thoughts and actions, you must **do what the ultimate model did – love people. Stop the hate**, the discrimination and bitterness. See them as He did – as God's children. This is the first thing that we all have in common. It doesn't matter if the other person is a different color, religion, or social class they have something that each of us can learn. Instead of seeing the differences, **look for**

similarities. This is how to **live in harmony** instead of constant battling with your own people. **Live as one**.

Imagine living a life that is full of opportunity. Look at every day as a new beginning – a challenge to use, not waste, God's gift. **Share your love and excitement** with other people. **Explore the world** of unlimited knowledge and experiences. It doesn't have to be the way that you are living now. The life you are living at this moment is because that is how you *think* you must live. You are seeing the situation through your customized lens that has been colored by your past programming. These programs are what you perceive as 'good' or 'bad.'

As I have said before, it takes guts to **leave the ruts.** It's not going to be easy to **do something different**. But until you have the guts to do it differently than you normally do, then everything will stay the same. Nothing is going to change until you **change.** The ball is in your court. You can either shoot or pass. The only way to score points is to step up and shoot. You might miss, but you won't know until you try. And even if you miss the first time, it's no big deal. You just keep practicing what you are trying to do and you eventually will **become a pro at it.**

When you **model a successful person** what should you be looking for? You should **find someone who is a <u>positive</u> Christian** – not just a reborn Christian. And there is a critical difference. A reborn Christian is one who has proclaimed Jesus Christ as their Savior. But, that is only a start. If it was that easy the world would not be as dark as it is today. The truth of the matter is there are many "reborn Christians" who are still being affected by negativity.

Learning how to live with the Positive Power of God is an ongoing quest. Negative thought patterns are NOT from God. You must not allow negative untruths such as resentment, bitterness, hard feelings, anger, hatred or ill will against another person to rule your life. These emotions will never allow you to feel your divine self.

A person cannot have God in their heart and have these pangs of darkness lurking in their personality. Just because a person has accepted Jesus Christ and the Holy Spirit and have made a commitment of living the Christian life, does not mean they are a positive Christian. Who can argue the point that too many Christians are living in negativity, jealousy, greed and hate? This is not the path that Jesus lived and he said 'follow me.'

The people you are searching for knows that to **walk in the footsteps of our Master** is a full-time commitment. It is a way of life. It is not just about being seen at church or tithing or reading your Bible. Yes, all of those things are important, but to truly manifest yourself into what every human being so desperately searches – to **be purified in thoughts and actions** you must not just **talk about Jesus** but you must **'do' Jesus.**

This enlightened person not only knows how to get things done, but is living the type of life that you want to live. These people **exist to help** and **love other humans** and they will help you **achieve your dreams**. The Positive Power of God and the manifestation of Jesus Christ can be seen on the faces of these blessed people. When you **feel the positive energy and love** from that special person you will know that you have found an enlightened one who will help you **resurrect yourself out of the darkness and into the light.**

"You call me Teacher and Lord; and you are right, for so I am..."

John 13:13

Thoughts are Things

"As he thinketh in his heart, so is he."

Proverbs 23:7

Most people don't **perceive thoughts as things**, but nonetheless, it is true. Thoughts are things. No, you can't touch or see them, but you can **feel and experience a thought**. What is a thought? Where does a thought originate? Why do we have the ability to think?

A thought is an electrical impulse that travels from the Divine Source of Intelligence – called God, to us through our mind. This burst of pure energy is much like the spark that the spark-plug in our cars produce. This God-like vibration is then conformed by our personal beliefs and attitude.

Picture the spark-plugs in your care misfiring (a negative thought). How far or fast do you think your car would travel? Most of us will agree that we wouldn't travel too far if our car engine was needing a tune up. If our personal spark-plugs are firing a positive message, we are "in tune" with God. We will **live in heaven every day** of our lives.

Our brain is constantly firing off either a negative or a positive spark of energy called a thought. Similar to a car engine, for our brain to run its absolute best, it must be firing a positive charge. The problem is, because of the barrage of negative pollution all of us encounter every day, we can't go very far in life without regular attitude "tune-ups".

Without daily positive adjustments, we become negatively programmed by the darkness, which continues getting worse, and eventually snuffs the life out of the most marvelous machine ever designed – the human mind.

The human mind needs a regular "tune-up" by the Positive Power of God so it can fire in a more constructive way. This is accomplished by learning and living the positive teachings of Jesus Christ. As the apostle Paul taught us, **"transform your life...by renewing your mind"**.

One is a member of the "walking dead" when their spiritual spark-plugs have burned out, which creates non-Christ thoughts. These poor souls ache to have their God-spark fanned with love and compassion. If you feel down and unloved you can **feel love again**. And it all begins with a positive thought. All you have to do is **have the faith to believe.**

There is nothing wrong about realizing and admitting you have lost your way. Much like Alcoholics Anonymous the first step of recovery is admittance. This awakening is much like recovery. No, it's not alcohol or drugs, but it is a condition that is as dangerous to the quality of your life.

When you've lost the spark of life, you have died. Sure, you're still existing but that's all. You're not having fun. You're not loving because first of all you don't **love yourself**. You can't love anybody else until you **love yourself.** And you won't **love yourself** until your thoughts are loving thoughts about yourself and others.

To **return to life** isn't hard. Actually, it's simple, but not easy. You must **change your thoughts**. If you want something different than what you are experiencing now, you have to **think different**. You can't expect something to change in your life without first changing how you think. I am positive that if you **change your thinking to a more loving thought**, your behavior will improve, which will **transform your life**. With every new thought and action there will be a new result.

This task might sound impossible but it's a simple process if you're willing to do it. If you have been experiencing a severely negative life, please **realize that you won't change overnight**. But the moment you **make the commitment to change**, you **start changing** immediately! The improvement starts out so small you are unable to see or **feel it**, but there is a change. It is impossible to **change your thoughts** and not change. It does take time, patience and the Positive Power of God. It is a new habit. And habits do take approximately thirty days to become a part of you.

Remember that thoughts are things. This means when an idea pops into your head, you can accept or not accept it – much like if someone was trying to give you a gift. If you don't want it, you can decline it; it's always your choice.

Don't be scared of your new outcome. Too many of us have attempted something in our lives and viewed the results as a failure. Because of this negative thinking, we quit trying. We do nothing. We choose the staleness of death over everlasting life. By choosing to do nothing we *have* decided to do something – nothing. And doing nothing is always going to get us the same result – death. Because of a negative thought, we have committed the ultimate sin – not using our God-given potential.

Are you committing the ultimate sin of refusing to **follow your chosen path?** This act of treason is like murdering your soul. You will never experience the mind-altering feeling that every human being experiences when their passion, which is sleeping deep inside them, explodes. You will never know this feeling unless you go for living your highest purpose.

It's so easy to get caught up in the trap which we call life. Life isn't what many people think. They only see an illusion that they believe is the truth. It isn't about having the most things. It *is* about doing the most with your God-given potential. This treasure that each of us possesses is so great, and it is hidden inside each of us.

Do you **remember when you were excited?** When every day was full of anticipation and passion? Why can't today be that way? The difference between that memorable day and today is our perception. We perceive ourselves as old and tired. Too many of us are negative thinkers.

As children we were positive thinkers and doers. We didn't let the word "can't" hold us back. As children we never used excuses and weren't afraid to try something new. No wonder Jesus tells us the only way to enter the Kingdom of Heaven is to be like a child – no negative thoughts, hang-ups, jealousy or prejudices. Kids just have fun, laugh, play, and use their imagination. That *would* be heaven, wouldn't it?

What happened? Are you afraid to come out of your comfort zone, which you've carefully established and built a fortress around? The same comfort zone that supposedly protects us from the violence of the world is suffocating us from the real life.

Our race has turned "anti-human". And this has happened because of negative thinking. The negativity of robbery, murder, rape, and stress has made us fear ourselves. Children are now being taught a new thought - "don't talk to strangers". I understand the reasoning, but this one thought programs our society to stay away from people who they don't know. This anti-social behavior limits the social skills of this person. It separates our race instead of bringing us closer together.

The answer is not to hide our head in our safety cocoons. It isn't contacting faceless souls on the Internet. The healing of your life comes down to expanding yourself and loving your neighbor. This act of freedom and kindness starts with your thought that you are thinking right now.

When you **live and love life to the fullest** you **resurrect yourself to the person you were designed to be** – strong, confident and positive. At this time, you **rediscover that hidden power** of deity. And to **receive all the blessings that God has planned for you,** you must **go for it**. What's the worst that can happen if you tried something new? You could lose money, have a failure, and embarrass yourself. So, what?

The worst is not going to kill you. And I know that you have heard the saying 'whatever doesn't kill you makes you stronger'. Whatever happens, you will be alive with more enthusiasm because you're dancing to your drummer. Sure, there will be scorners who will call you foolish for doing something you want to do. But don't let them fool you. Some of them will be envious of your courage to **do something for yourself**.

I have experienced 'death' before more than once. I felt the angel of death upon my face whenever I ached through the motions of working a job that I had no passion and knew was not my correct path. I didn't try to dislike my new position. Yet, despite my efforts, I was always inwardly scolded how this asn't the correct use of my time. And I must admit that during those job-searching tantrums, I felt lost – like a hobo drifting from work place to job site, secretly knowing what my true mission was, and having to **find the courage to pursue it**.

Are you petrified to **take the plunge** – not having the faith in yourself or God to really do what you **know in your heart He is telling you** is the right thing to do? Why is it always so scary to do **what feels right**? Remember the saying "if it feels good, **do it**". But many of us have been programmed no to **do the things that feel good** because they were supposedly wrong.

The first time I felt this Divine discontent was when I was married to my first wife. Everything had been laid out on a silver platter for me – a house; cars; business and money. But I quickly learned that when you have a bigger mission you will **feel the message**. I would never be where I am today, doing the work that I am destined to accomplish, if I had not felt that dissatisfaction and had the courage to take action to **change the situation.**

Don't get me wrong, I'm not saying to be unhappy. There is a huge difference between being unhappy and discontented. Unhappiness is an attitude of not looking at your situation as a blessing. Discontent means that you are happy with life but are not satisfied with what you have accomplished. You feel an uneasiness inside- a need to do more. Divine discontent drives you to the next higher plateau in the consciousness of life. This unrest in your soul is speaking to you. Are you listening?

You are the only one who knows if you feel these uncomfortable feelings. These disturbing thoughts and feelings are Divine messages telling you that something isn't complete in your life. You are not in alignment with your life purpose. If you do **sense these sensations** then the ultimate power of God is talking to you. And when it happens it is very hard to stop its persistence. The feeling starts small, like an itch, but grows and becomes infectious, leading to the passion that engulfs your soul and moves you along your path to a state of higher consciousness.

Think of something you have done in your life at which you were very adept. You are confident in this endeavor and feel sure of yourself in your abilities to perform this particular task. Did you always feel this confident? Of course not. Why? In the beginning of developing this acquired skill, you didn't know anything about what you now have vast knowledge. It took time, patience and experience to become a master at your skill.

Your spiritual and personal growth is no different. When you first started this task that you are now an 'expert' you probably never dreamed you would be as good as you are now. As a human becoming, you don't **realize how powerful you actually are**. Every one of us is blessed with a Divine force. Your challenge is to **believe, find** and **use this incredible power.** As Star Wars taught us – May the Force Be With You!

"We truly can do anything that we believe we can do." After hearing this statement from the teacher, a student challenged the wise master; "but master, I can't move a mountain." The master answered "I know.". The confused student asked the wiser one again, "so then how can you teach such an untruthful statement?" The enlightened one responded "I am not the one stating the untruth. Everything that you and I said are true. The conflict between these two statements is only one thing – a thought. I promised you that you could do anything you believed you could do. That statement is true. You don't *believe* you can move a mountain, so your statement is also true."

You will always **reap what you sow.** If you entertain a negative, limiting thought you will be limiting your possibilities. If you **plant positive thoughts** they will blossom into a harvest of abundance.

Jesus said "He that believeth in me, the words that I do shall he do also; and greater works than these shall he do..." (John 14:12). Think what this means – according to the Bible. What did Jesus do? He performed miracles. Scripture promises you that you can **perform miracles.** And I believe the first miracle that each of us can perform is the resurrection of a new life for ourselves. We have the Divine Power in each of us. It is only a thought away.

In college I was introduced to the following story, which I would like to share with you;

A Hindu legend states that all men were deity at one time. But because they abused their power, Brahma, the chief god, ordered that man be stripped of this divine power. It would be hidden where man could never find it. The other gods were called in by Brahma to suggest ideas about where to hide man's divine power. The first god suggested, "Let's bury man's divinity deep in the earth."

Brahma said "no, that is not good because man will dig deep into the earth and find it."

The second god proudly announced, "I know the perfect place. We will sink man's treasure into the deepest part of the ocean."

"That will not do either. Man will explore the deepest depths of the ocean and discover his divine power."

The third god suggested, "Let's place it on the highest mountain peak. There, we can hide the divinity of man."

"No. Man will scale to the highest mountain tops and would discover their hidden treasure." Finally, Brahma announced "I know the perfect place – somewhere man will never look. We will hide it deep inside him. He will never think about looking so close."

Ever since the beginning of time, man has searched, hunted, dug and explored for that one thing to fill that feeling of emptiness. The power of God that is in each of us has been the best kept secret in all the ages. The answer is so close, yet so far because it is only a thought away.

Man's eternal quest should be inner space. This is the most interesting and promising area that is still left unexplored. Hidden away in each of us is a vast gold mine, waiting to be discovered and mined. And what is remarkable about this reserve of riches is that you can't ever spend it all. It is the true "pot of gold at the end of the rainbow"; the fountain of youth and the answer to every problem or challenge that you face. This treasure chest of personal power is just waiting for you to **discover it** and **use it** to its full potential.

It is not the talents we possess, but rather our attitude about those talents. Our weakness is our lack of belief. We, as humans and as God's creation, have infinite potential. Many of us are on this quest, searching for happiness and success, only to **discover the Truth** that this Ultimate power is inside each and every one of us.

So now the "secret" is out. What secret? The path to enrichment, happiness and success has been preached, taught and studied for thousands of years. The formula is simple, yet the results are disastrous. I have not given you new information. You possess all the knowledge that you need in order to be great. I am only the messenger to

awaken the sleeping giant and show you how to **bring these talents and gifts to the surface** and **make them a reality.** I hope I have stated these words in a manner in which you not only enjoyed reading, but more importantly inspired you to **act upon your thoughts**. If you don't **respond to these words** then we have both wasted our time. By not using this knowledge to **better your life and the world,** it is no better than if you had never laid eyes upon this work.

I am absolutely certain that these words can improve every human's life if, and only if, the reader tears down the wall of negativity that has engulfed them. **Listen not to those negative thoughts** that try to dominate your thinking. **Push them out of your head. Don't let those disempowering ideas hold you prisoner. Try implementing these ideas into your life**.

Since you have continued reading this far, you truly desire to **break out of your death sentence of mediocrity; to escape the programming of being "average". Get mad. Get motivated. Fight to get your life back.** There is nothing more important or challenging than living with a positive thought. Don't let even one moment slip through your fingers. **Take control of your thoughts** immediately. **Seize control of your mind** and you will **control your life**. **Seize the day!**

Last but not least, **think where you are going to be in five... ten.... twenty years** from today... if you don't change. Is that where you want to be? If the future looks bright and you are feeling passionate about it then that is the path for you. But if you are like many people, looking into the future you might not like what you see. Then what?

The only way that your future is going to change is if you **decide** that you're hurting enough to really change – **take immediate action** and **do something to resurrect yourself.** Every action starts with a thought. **Start now. Imagine what you want to be, do, and have.** What would you like to leave behind? How would you like to **make this world a better place** for your children and their children? What was your life about? How would you like the world to remember you?

Think. What God-given talent do you possess? What do you **have a passion** about? How can you **design a living around the strengths which you possess? Start there**. Don't negative thoughts go through your head. They are the tyrants that try to steal your dreams and stop you from fulfilling God's plan for you.

Yes, thoughts are things. They are the things that motivate or demotivate you. They **control your life**. Thoughts make you what you are or are not. Thoughts are the beginning or the end, the alpha or the omega. **Make sure your thoughts are the same as the ones Jesus thought** – positive, empowering thoughts that can **create the miracle of resurrection** not only for you, but for the world.

"O sing to the Lord a new song."

Psalms 33:3

Being Balanced in an Unbalanced World

"For what will it profit a man if he gains the whole world and forfeits his life?"

Matthew 16:26

Picture yourself as an Olympic athlete. Can you **see it**? Come on – **imagine**. You're performing on the balance beam. You make a vault and miss your mark. In that instant, you know you're in trouble. You **feel yourself out of balance**. You get scared, mad and stressed.

Because of the abrupt change, the brain has set into action the emotion of fear (fight or flight). You receive extra mental power; a surge of adrenaline rushes through your system. For a split second you have the choice to **regain your balance** or let fear knock you off the beam.

If you do fall off the beam – and sometimes that is going to happen, do you **get up and try again** until you **learn** how to do that move with balance, or do you give up? This choice makes all the difference.

All of us have our own balance beam called life. Every person feels this unbalanced feeling the second they stray from their God-given path. The moment you are not living in the now you will know it. Once we become unbalanced by yesterday's guilt or tomorrow's fear, stress starts attacking our bodies, wearing us down and keeping us away from God. To **remove the pain and suffering** we must **live in the present moment** being more aware of life and grateful for each and every breath.

Think of balance as a wheel that is perfectly round. Much like your car's wheels, when the tire is full inflated your ride is smooth, effortless, and at the speed that you choose. But, let a tiny piece of glass or sharp nail come into contact with your tire and your world can **change instantly**. This is how life is. At birth, our "wheels" are balanced and fully inflated, ready to travel the journey of life. Through our early years our wheels roll smoothly, protecting us from the bumps. But slowly, they start to wear. We have all experienced wheels getting out of balance as we drive our cars. When we feel this uncomfortable vibration we take it to our local mechanic and get the front end of our car aligned. But, when our bodies start feeling negative vibrations we procrastinate, believing it will automatically get better. We take better care of our car than we do our own bodies; our true vehicle in which we experience this voyage.

Our brain is a wonderful receiver and transmitter that automatically tells us immediately when there is something out of balance. It communicates to us through the sense of pain. Besides obvious physical pain, there is emotional/psychological pain. This mental imbalance causing stress is because of 'wrong thinking.' To relieve stress, you must **get your system back into balance** and it all starts in the brain and how we think.

The act of balancing is an inner mental game. Balance has nothing to do with the rest of the world. It is not "their" fault you feel the way you feel. As humans we are always trying to blame someone else. To **regain your balance** you must **take full responsibility** and **do something about it.**

Every person has eight areas that must be balanced. These include:

Mental – This balance point is the north point of the axis. This area includes the person's attitude – whether they are positive or negative, their beliefs and values and aptitude. A person is what s/he thinks and will become whatever they focus on. A positive thought pattern, empowering beliefs and an increasing aptitude will support balance and peace of mind. Negative thoughts, disempowering beliefs or a closed mind will plummet the person into an unbalanced life of disharmony, havoc and unhappiness.

<u>Spiritual</u> – Too many motivational self-help books lack spiritual knowledge. This area is many times blocked by negative beliefs and a closed mind. In many instances, religion has created fear and imbalance in this area. When you **experience the truth** you will **know the truth**. Once this truth is experienced and practiced, this balance area will grow and help all other areas come into balance. Without this area balanced, it is impossible to achieve true, complete balance.

<u>Family</u> – This is one of the hardest areas to balance because there are always other people involved. To create balance in this sector you must **remember the law that you can only change yourself.** Family can be difficult. I thank God that we have a loving bond within our family. Family is an important part of the first chakra – the tribal energy. It is important to *belong*. It is a shame that so many families have distanced themselves from one another. By this action, all who are involved will become more out of

harmony, which is going away from God. We must **mend the broken pieces** of our families. We must **forgive and forget**. We must **stand up, hold hands and be strong** – as one family. The best way to **balance this area**, as with the rest of them, is to **do a little at a time.** Always try to **do your best** with the thought of love behind it. It might not always work but at least you'll feel better. You won't have guilt. Guilt is a negative emotion that throws us out of balance. There is more guilt in this area of the wheel than in any other. More people have problems with their families than in any other area of concern. **Do what you can. Pray for them. Give them your love. Hand it over to God** and let the all-knowing energy of the Almighty work His miracles. And when you **believe with all your heart and soul**, it will happen.

Relationships – This area is not only about your love life. It can be about many types of relationships in which you are involved. All of us are involved in different types of relationships, and each of these presents a challenge. Negativity in any of these partnerships can create an imbalance that can affect the rest of your life. The closer the relationship, the stronger the effect of the energy on you. Ones in which you are involved on a daily basis are much stronger than a once-a-year meeting. Of course, ones that have an immediate impact on your life are the most powerful. Examples would be your love life, your boss at work and your children. Every relationship does affect your balancing act. The first step of balancing this area is to use the Wheel of Balance and evaluate a relationship that you feel is in question. A relationship that you don't feel comfortable with is the first one you should take action towards rebalancing.

Relationships, much like family, are sometimes difficult because you cannot change anyone other than yourself. So again, you must realize that you can do everything humanly possible, and if the benefactor does not respond in a positive way then you must make the choice to either continue a relationship that influences you in a negative way or break it off. I understand that this is much easier said than done, but it is possible if you truly believe that you can. **Ask for guidance** and **take action** with the thought of love in your heart.

Physical Health – Too many of us take our bodies for granted – until something goes wrong. I absolutely **believe**

that health is wealth. The problem with most of us is that keeping the body in top form takes work and discipline. All of us know how important it is to eat a healthy diet, get enough rest, exercise, and keep a positive attitude. But how many of us **put out the extensive effort to accomplish this daily challenge.**

Our body is such a wonderful machine that the Bible states it could live productively for 120 years. But, because of our habits, thoughts, and poisoning of our bodies, we wear our 'vehicle for life' out. If you don't realize how important your health really is, visit a nursing home. If that doesn't wake you up, nothing will. Just tell yourself that if you don't take care of your body, you could end up trapped; sitting in a wheelchair, waiting for your medication, having to have someone feed you and change you. It is a disgusting picture of getting older. Use this powerful image to motivate you to better health. But it doesn't have to be that way.

Jack LaLane, 89 years young, still starts every morning at 5:30am with an hour of exercise. Some people believe being healthy when we get older is luck or genes. But, every effort you make toward your health and well-being is another minute of good health you are buying. Everything you do to harm your body steals a precious second of your life. Balancing your physical health is not easy, but it is crucial in order to achieve true success. Too many clients we work with believe they are successful because they have money, but fail to realize that without health, they have nothing. There is an abundance of information on how to get in better physical condition. But here are some pointers:

Breathing – One of our teachers told us a story of when she had the honor to speak with Tibetan monks. When it was her turn, one of the monks asked her the question "what is life?" She answered once, but not to their satisfaction. So another echoed the famous question "what is life?" After failing to arrive at the answer they desired of her, they enlightened her - "life is breath". Breathing is the most crucial act we do to survive, yet we hardly **spend a second thinking about this life-sustaining process**. So important and needed, but because it is so constant, we take it for granted. But if you will **invest some attention into the art of breathing**, you will **see amazing results**.

Most people breathe in a shallow manner; only using the top part of their lungs, which is the smallest area of the lungs. This limited lung capacity, and the reduction of the oxygen content in the air that we are inhaling, cuts down the oxygen intake, which is the most important element needed by our bodies to run efficiently. Less oxygen entering our bodies starts a slow process of deterioration, disease, aging and death.

To **learn how to breathe properly**, study yoga. If you don't do this important step, then at least begin with a deep-breathing exercise of 1 – 4 – 2. These numbers represent the seconds you hold each step of the breathing process. Before starting your count, you must first understand how to make sure you are accomplishing deep breathing. The easiest technique is to fold both your hands over your stomach. Take in a breath. If you are deep breathing, your hands will be pushed out by your stomach muscles. If you are still breathing in a shallow manner, you will feel your shoulders go up as you are trying to get more air in. Practice until you can make your hands move out and then use the method described below.

The first step is to inhale. Count seconds while breathing in through your nostrils until you cannot hold any more air. The next step is to hold. You hold your breath for a count of 4 times the number of seconds you inhaled. For example, if you inhaled for 8 seconds, you would hold for 32 seconds. This holding time is very important because it starts your lymph system working, cleaning out more toxins than all exercise. The third step is to exhale. Breathe out comfortably until you have pushed out all of the air. This should take twice as long as inhaling, so using our example above, it would be 8 seconds times 2, which would be 16 seconds.

Try to do this in the morning and evening. It is a great midday pick up. By doing this exercise, your body will receive much-needed oxygen. If you can **do 10 repetitions at least once a day** for thirty days, you will **feel like a new person**! One cautionary; if you start feeling dizzy or ill feeling stop immediately with the deep breathing exercise.

Diet – There is so much information that is contradictory about eating, who knows what is right? One food is in, then it's out, and something new has taken its place. Then there are the fad diets. This week you eat all protein; another week all chocolate; the next week, who knows? People will do anything to lose weight, except take the time to do it right.

First of all, **don't ever go on a diet again**. The first three letters are DIE, after all. **Learn how to combine food** for the best digestion. A teacher once taught me to **eat like a king for breakfast**, a prince for lunch, and a pauper for supper. If you **take this advice** and **follow the no eating after 6pm** rule, you will be on your way.

<u>Emotion</u> – This area of The Balance Wheel is so important because if we allow them to, emotions will control our lives. I believe that all of us have to admit that our "emotions" have gotten us in trouble. But what are emotions? According to the American College Dictionary, emotion is "a state of mind in which one experiences joy, sorrow, fear, hate or love". It is a feeling. Emotions are not necessarily good or bad. Emotions are emotions- energy in motion. It seems like women are more emotional than men. In some ways this might be good, but there are ways this is detrimental in terms of a male being able to express himself. A person who is described as "too emotional" cannot usually face certain situations without getting "emotionally involved". On the other side of the coin, some people do not show their emotions at all, and cannot truly express themselves.

All of us have emotions – positive emotions like love, joy and compassion, and negative emotions like hate, fear and jealousy. Ask yourself as you complete the Wheel of Balance, if your emotions are bringing you closer to God – peace of mind and love (10). Or are they tossing you around in the ocean of life, much like a drop of water in a breaking wave?

<u>Career</u> – Straight across The Balance Wheel from family is career. These opposites are a constant struggle for many people. "How can I become successful in business and have time with my family?" Most of the time when the career needs more attention, the time is always taken from the family. Because of having to make this choice, many career-minded people quickly becomes unbalanced which produces stress, which turns to unhappiness, anger and burnout. They become members of the "walking dead".

A balance of career and family is possible. Corporations are changing slowly. Males are feeling the importance of being more "hands-on" when it comes to fatherhood. Men are taking a more active role in raising their children. There are many changes in the work force that will help individuals to regain balance in this area. But, it is each individual's choice of what is most important to them.

Financial – Last, but by no means least, is the subject of money. This area is important to most people, and all of us understand why. If you don't agree, I challenge you to try living without money. You will quickly **experience the power of money** in our materialistic society. We must **find a delicate balance** as Paul stated; "**be in this world but not of this world**".

I have experienced both ends of the money spectrum. I have lived with a good cash flow, and I have teetered on the brink of bankruptcy. Believe me, having money in your pocket is always better. Yes, money is worshipped in our society, whether we want to admit it or not. But it doesn't have to rule our lives. Sure, money is important. But not more important than any other area on The Balance Wheel. Money is an energy, that's all. This energy can be used in a positive or negative way. Money moves in directions of least resistance. It also follows the Law of Nature of "Like Attracts Like". Since money is an energy, it will move toward another energy. If you produce energy (movement) toward a cause of helping your fellow human being, you will be rewarded. To accomplish using money instead of money using you, you must stay balanced. God wants us to **be abundant**, but you have to **do what you can do to help your finances** along. There are many good programs concerning finance. You should **read**, **study** and **implement these wise and proven techniques**.

The goal of The Balance Wheel is to bring awareness to the eight areas of your life and to bring attention to the specific areas in which you are out-of-balance so you can improve your life. These are the areas of your life that you have control of through the power of choice. If you can honestly admit that you need help rebalancing an area, this program can start you toward a step-by-step healing process - if you choose.

This exercise is a self-evaluation. Taking it should be your choice, and yours alone. Nobody should ever be forced to participate. This personal inventory will be as helpful as your answers are true. There are no right or wrong answers. Your answers are always right unless they are wrong – and the only reason they would be wrong is if you did not write down the right answers.

On the following page, **look at <u>The Wheel of Balance</u>**. Notice there is a small circle in the middle. That represents YOU. **Read Step One to understand the evaluation system**. Then **mark your answer** on the corresponding number in each section. When you are finished, you should have eight dots. Step Two is connecting the dots to **form one continuous shape**. The goal of this shape is a perfect circle. The question is, what does your 'circle' look like? Has it got a flat spot or is it lumpy? Maybe it is deflated on one side or the other. **Find the flat spot on your balance wheel** and **start immediately with that area**. Once you **see your areas of concern** it is now time to **put into full effect what you have learned in <u>Resurrecting Your Life.</u>**

Use your imagination and **dream of the result that would have to happen to move your evaluation out by one mark**. What would it take, in your opinion, to move this part of your life from (1) feeling hopeless, to a (2) terrible, and continue until you have worked that area closer to balance. You **make this movement by using the steps in this book – dream, set goals, and take action.** Once you **believe you have advanced to that level**, then **ask**

yourself what it will take to advance to the next level, and the next....

Achieving balance in an unbalanced world is not easy. And it is impossible to attempt it alone. Remember the poem, "Footprints in the Sand". God is with you always. He never leaves you. And through those hard times, it's important we have someone who will support and protect us. All things are possible with God.

The Wheel of Balance is a tool for you to **critique your life**. Balance is possible. A person who makes the excuse that they don't have time to **achieve balance**, needs it the most. Every human being is on this earth to **experience a marvelous journey**, but God has given each of us the freedom to travel as we choose. If you would rather have a smoother, less tiring trip, and become truly successful, **start getting your life in balance. Start today by doing the following exercise** – The Wheel of Balance.

THE WHEEL OF BALANCE

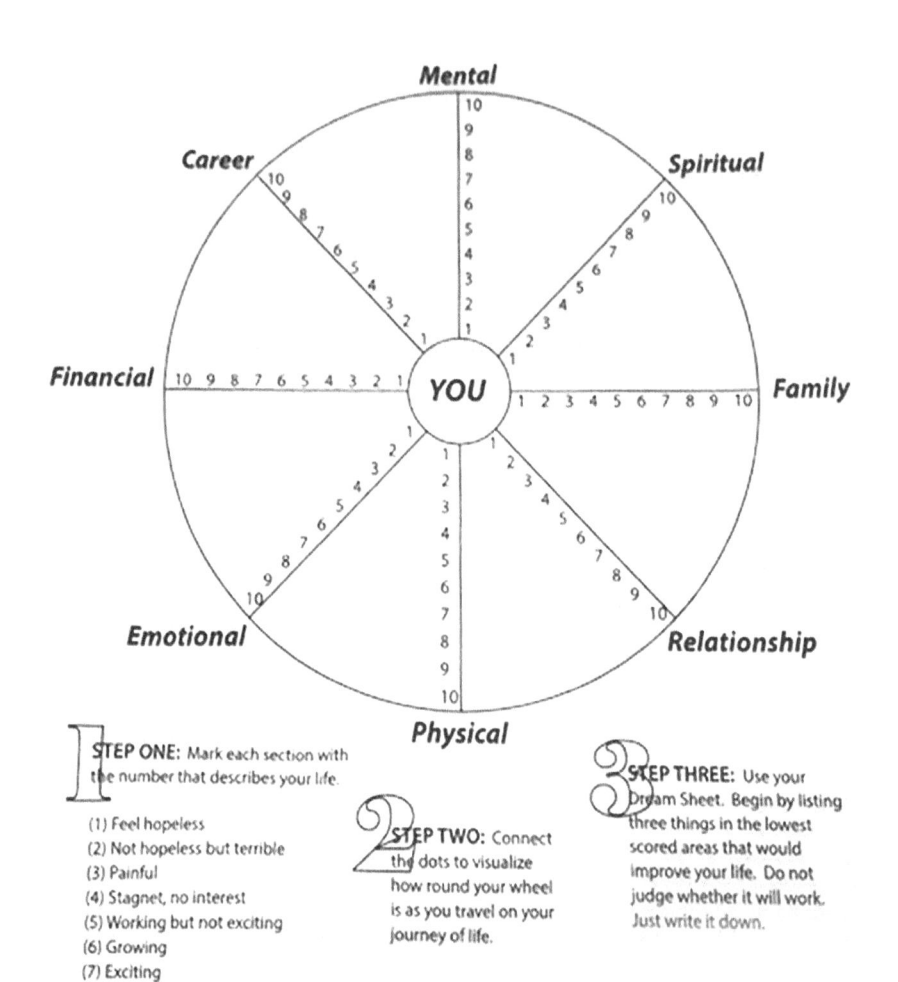

Mental • **Spiritual** • **Family** • **Relationship** • **Physical** • **Emotional** • **Financial** • **Career**

YOU

STEP ONE: Mark each section with the number that describes your life.

(1) Feel hopeless
(2) Not hopeless but terrible
(3) Painful
(4) Stagnet, no interest
(5) Working but not exciting
(6) Growing
(7) Exciting
(8) High energy area
(9) Almost perfect
(10) = Perfect

STEP TWO: Connect the dots to visualize how round your wheel is as you travel on your journey of life.

STEP THREE: Use your Dream Sheet. Begin by listing three things in the lowest scored areas that would improve your life. Do not judge whether it will work. Just write it down.

copyright Mind-o-VallioN 1997

The Greatest Story Ever Told

"Truth is the most valuable thing we have"

Mark Twain

There is always an end to every beginning and a beginning to every end. The Bible states that 'this too shall pass'. Our time together is about to expire. Our paths have crossed for a purpose. I believe that my life purpose is to share with you the love I have for this energy of infinite intelligence many of us call God. Also, to **awaken the sleeping giant** that is waiting to help you **perform your chosen task with more enthusiasm, energy and excitement** than you ever thought possible! My mission is to tell you that your life can be the greatest story ever told...once you **discover your God-given power**.

Have you caught the fever yet? I have contemplated endlessly on the perfect words that will do the trick – **turn the key that unlocks your Godliness**. Do you **feel differently** than before you started reading this book? I pray that you read this far, and didn't skip ahead, like I have to confess I do sometimes. If you **feel better; have more**

hope; think new ideas or can now **see the proverbial light at the end of the tunnel**, you have felt the truth of the Positive Power of God. You have experienced a small sample of God's awesomeness. You have felt the warmth and comfort of the white light. And the only way to fully **understand the truth** is to **experience it**.

This is the end of a project with which I've had a love/hate relationship. It's been a challenge in which I have invested many years of my life – to take words and ideas of twenty-five years of studying many of the great teachers and place on these pages my interpretation of the living truth. It is now time for you to **take these words** which I have carefully written and **use them as tools** to **make your life the most fulfilling** you can humanly achieve. That is the reason you picked this book, isn't it? To **heal yourself, make yourself feel better,** to **be the person God desires you to be?** And the great news is... you can **do it** and you can **start right now!**

An elderly gentleman once taught me; "never do anything because you *have* to; **do it because you *want* to, and know it is the right thing to do.**" This book is the epitome of his words. I've enjoyed the process. However, it's more important for you to **take these words** and **use them** to not just make a living but **think enough of yourself to design your life.**

The only thing that would make me happier than having the opportunity of writing Resurrecting Your Life would be you letting me know that this information changed your life. In Mark O. Haroldsen's book, The Courage to Be Rich, the author refers to the "IGDS Philosophy". This acronym is the reminder: "**I**'m **G**oing to **D**ie **S**omeday". And then he asks why not really **go for happiness, health and abundance**? What do you have to lose?

I worked as a hairdresser for over twenty years of my life. I talked to thousands of clients. The majority of them visited me to not only look their best, but also to feel great. I spent hundreds of hours counseling my clients under the auspices of hairdressing, and loved every minute of this extra, personal service. One day I explained to a top corporate executive, who was a client of mine, my reasoning of what I was doing – I was going for it. I explained to him that hairdressing had brought me to that particular level of my life. I was grateful for what it had done for me. I loved making people look handsome and beautiful, but the truth of the matter was my higher purpose was motivating and inspiring audiences to live their God-given potential and to help them heal.

I had to go through a healing time myself – almost five years after my ultimate challenge, before I was ready. But I now knew that the time was perfect for the biggest challenge in my life – helping **change the world** by teaching natural health using the Positive Power of God to **share with people how to heal**.

I had to come to the realization of truth, that I had to first **master the art of loving** myself so I could **truly love others**. Don't let that 'hardening of the attitudes' harden your heart. **Have compassion for yourself first**.

As you have read throughout this book, the power that I am writing about is not outside somewhere. It is inside each of us. A person who searches beyond themselves for the answers will only find fool's gold, but the ones who look inside are those who are awakened. Now is the time to **begin your journey of self-discovery. Start immediately**. Don't let any excuses get in your way. **Don't delay** even one more minute. **Do it now.** You'll never be sorry that you followed your heart's desire.

To **resurrect yourself**, you must **take action**. Don't be like the couch athlete that sits back and watches as the game is being played. Jump in with both feet. **Start small** but **be committed. Be a player in the game of life.** This is the alpha and omega of your life. You can never go back to where you were before you read this book. Your mind has been expanded.

You now **know more**, but the question is: will you **use the new information?** Do you **have enough faith** and belief to **change yourself?** Will you **face the unknown future with positive expectancy** or negative nonsense? Don't be like the college graduate who becomes a professional student for the wrong reason – staying in his comfort zone and not having to **face the 'big bad' world. Step out. Have courage**. Jesus says, "**Be bold. Be brave.**"

Being resurrected from the dead starts your new awakening. The purpose of life is having a life of purpose. As long as you **live a purposeful life** with the Positive Power of God, you will **live a heavenly life.** The minute that you lose the purpose that you have worked so hard to distinguish throughout this book, you start dying again. Don't allow the darkness of negativity to invade your garden. The Positive Power of God will always win. Always!

By this time, I pray that you are taking baby steps toward your God-given dream. Remember this most important concept; you don't have to wait to **accomplish your dream** to live God's great life. All you have to do is **work on accomplishing something daily** toward your dreams, in the name of love.

If you don't know how to **get started,** but **know inside that you need to change, do what the scriptures tell us;** "**Be still** and **know that I am God**".

Never underestimate the power of prayer, meditation and silence. Everything starts as a a divine seed of an idea that you **feel passionate** about. **Ask yourself what you excel at**, and what makes you happy. **Start there**, by asking how you can **turn your passion into a living**.

Don't think you have to jump off the deep end. As a matter of fact, I don't suggest doing it like I did. I got kicked out of the nest. It felt like I had been shoved off of a cliff and I didn't know if I was going to fly or crash. But with God's help, we flew. With the Positive Power of God, you won't crash, but you have to **do something** before God will help you **design your new life.**

When you **study the miracles of Jesus.** He always had the person **do something** before the miracle could be performed. The servants were asked to fill vases with water, and then serve it as the finest wine – and the water was served with faith and it was the best wine of the wedding. You are no different. You must **have the faith and belief** and **demonstrate this faith by taking action.**

Benny Hinn confesses in his books that he never knows beforehand that he will have the power of the anointing. He must **act in faith** and **believe** that the anointing of God will come through him. And because of his perfect faith, he places his hand against the sick, and they are shown the power of God.

If you will **prove your faith with action** it is impossible for you not to succeed. God does not make failures and that includes you. It doesn't matter what you have done or haven't done, your task can be manifested through the name of Jesus Christ and the Positive Power of God.

Go now. **Take these lessons and use them.** <u>Resurrecting Your Life</u> is not about whether you're going to heaven or hell after you die or whether you've been saved or not. These areas are concerns of all of us and I believe they are being addressed by our churches. But, I believe that we worry so much about where we are going after we die, that we are not focusing on what we are doing with God's great gift NOW. **Learn to live "in-the-now". Experience life** with all six senses. The only way that you're going to experience the heaven that you are looking for, is to **live as if** you are there right now. It starts with a higher consciousness – Christ-consciousness.

If you **live the life that Jesus lived, think the thoughts that Jesus thought**, and **have the faith to take action** like Jesus every day of your life, then you have truly found the answer. Yes, confessing that Jesus died for your sin is a call of faith, yet living the life that Jesus demonstrated and died for is truly giving your life to Jesus Christ. You have made a true commitment to God when you **walk in Jesus' sandals, speak His words** and **spread the great Word** throughout your path toward helping your fellow man. As we all know, actions speak louder than words.

Don't be scared. Just **follow your passion. Take action**. If your heart's deepest desire is the miracle of resurrecting yourself out of the woes of a living death, then **take that leap of faith**. As I stated earlier, every miracle that Jesus performed, He first asked the person to take a step in faith. What is going to be your first step toward working God's miracle? To perform your own miracle, you must take action. Don't wait for God to do something.

Do your work in God's name and you will **be happy** and successful. **Do all things with love** and compassion. Yes, it is true that the truth will set you free. And the truth is - you can **rise above the problems** in your life. You can **be more** than you are now. You can **be a member of God's great team**. You are made in the image of God.

Now all you have to do is **go out into the world** and **share your God-given talents** and gifts. **Do it with the energy of love** and your life will be the greatest story ever told.

It is indeed possible to bring to earth as it is in heaven. We perceive heaven to be pure, loving and positive. Why do we have to die to experience such a place? Each of us has the choice to live in heaven or hell, every second of our lives. Love is the obvious answer. Why has the message been so distorted? The answer is simple. As the song says **"let there be peace on earth**, and **let it begin with you"**.

"Whatever is true, whatever is honorable, whatever is just, whatever is pleasing, whatever is commendable, if there is any excellence and if there is anything worthy of praise, **think about these things...**

Philippians 4:8

...and you will **be resurrected**.

AFTERTHOUGHTS

Resurrection can come at any time in your life, no matter how dark the night appears.

Death is not the enemy; the fear of death is. To truly resurrect oneself is to **face the fear** of death and then one can **live the truth**.

All human stress corresponds with a spiritual imbalance or crisis. The first step on the journey of resurrection is to **become harmonious with God**.

To resurrect oneself, one must be able to **evaluate what is no longer true**, and **change that which is not.**

The act of resurrection requires a unity of mind, body and soul as one. Asking yourself the question; "for what purpose was I created?" will guide you to your personal transformation.

Resurrection comes from your inner world, not the outer. Resurrection is reuniting with God – with love in every facet of your life.

The need to revive or resurrect ourselves is created every moment we wander away from God by thinking a negative thought.

You are the only one who can **perform the miracle of resurrecting yourself**. It is your own "cross to bear".

Every crisis is an opportunity to **resurrect yourself** by choosing the highest choice – the one that Jesus would have chosen.

Make the choice – choose to live again with the powerful, positive passion of being all God planned for you to be and then you will be blessed and living a heavenly life. **Read <u>Resurrecting Your Life</u>** and **put its words into your life**, and you will **find the truth**; and the truth shall set you free!

<u>Resurrecting Your Life</u> can help you **live the life that you have dreamed** and God has planned for you. Its purpose is to **give hope and inspiration** to every person who has died at heart and feels the emptiness of "Divine Discontent".

<u>Resurrecting Your Life</u> is based from Jesus' teachings. He was the first Holistic Health Coach, and his time-proven teachings are as valuable today as they were 2,000 years ago.

This "Holistic Health Coaching Manual" can help you **have your own personal resurrection.** It will teach and motivate you to **take back your life** through the Positive Power of God and the words of Jesus Christ.

ABOUT THE AUTHOR

Dr. Jerry Weber, N.D.

Dr. Jerry Weber is a board-certified Naturopath doctor and Holistic Health Coach who specializes in helping people heal naturally. He is the co-creator of The Body Balance Healing System, which is a proven system of natural health care utilizing muscle testing. He has tested thousands of patients by using this system.

Dr. Weber has been involved in 'the human potential movement' for over thirty years. He believes that the body can heal itself if the flow of energy is balanced in the areas of physical, emotional, mental and spiritual areas. He has dedicated his life in helping people learn how to take better care of their body, mind and spirit.

Dr. Weber's practice is at Health and Wellness of Carmel in Carmel, Indiana. He lives in Columbus, Indiana with his wife – Ann, and their dog, Rocky.

CONTACT INFORMATION:

www.hwofc.com

drjerome56@yahoo.com

You Tube – Dr. Jerry Weber

Blogs:

    Health Truths Revealed

    Journey of A Naturopath